freehand

recent works by

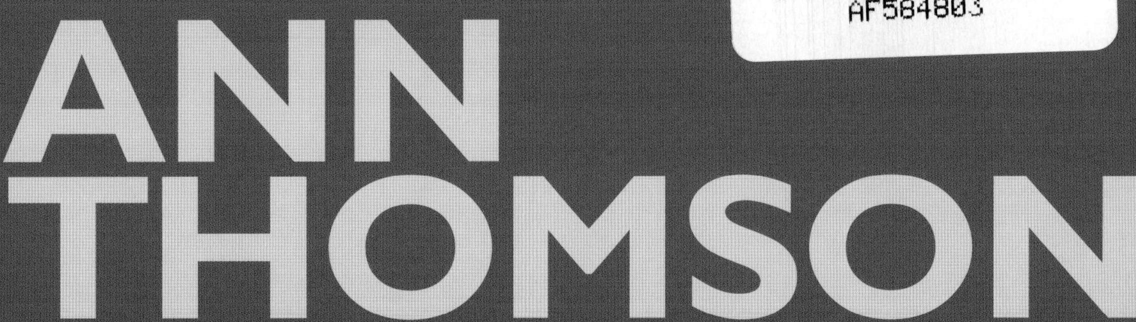

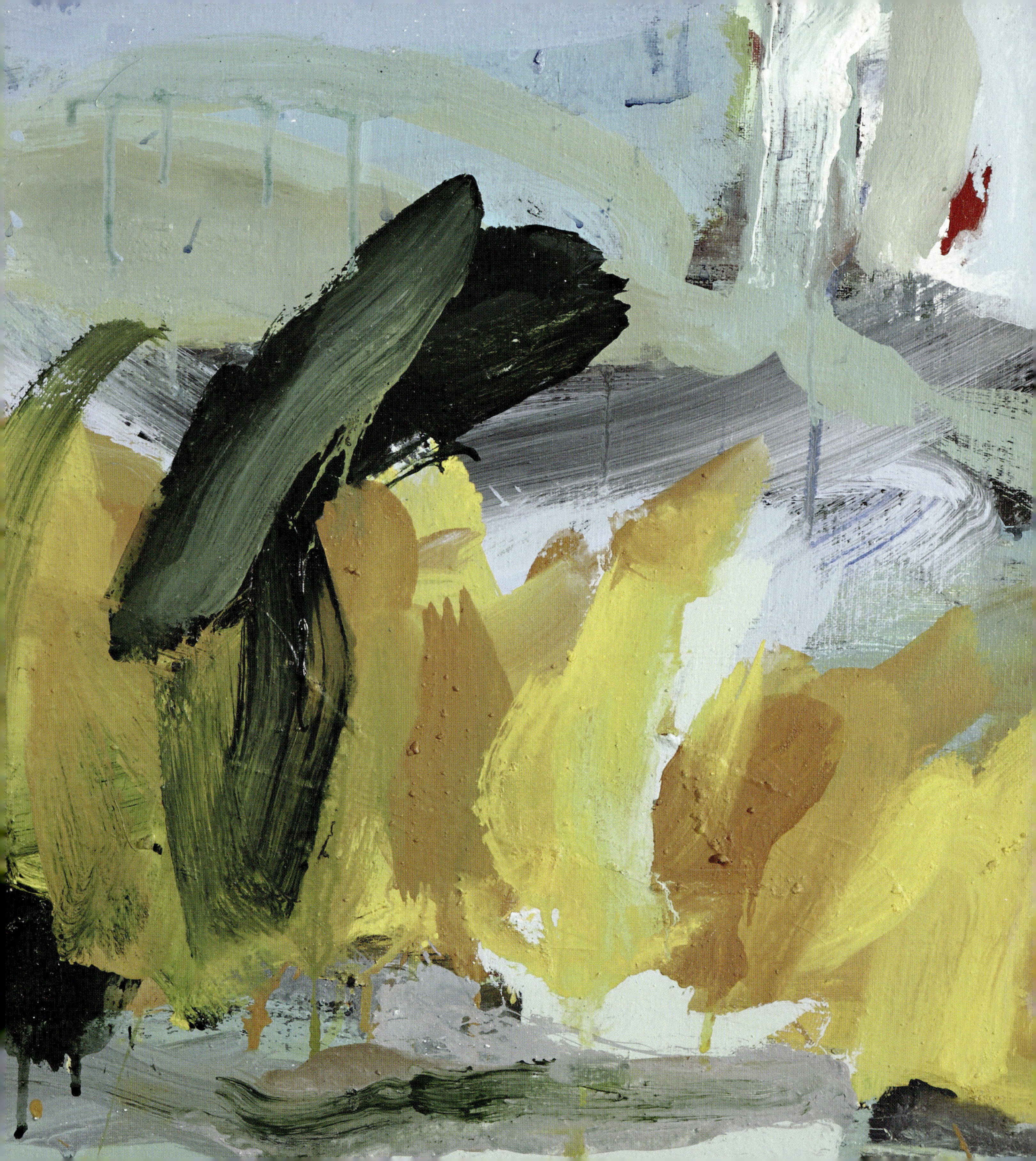

contents

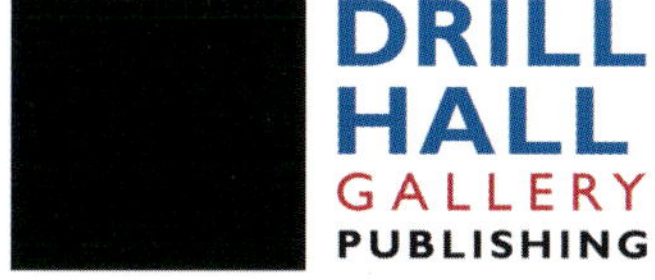

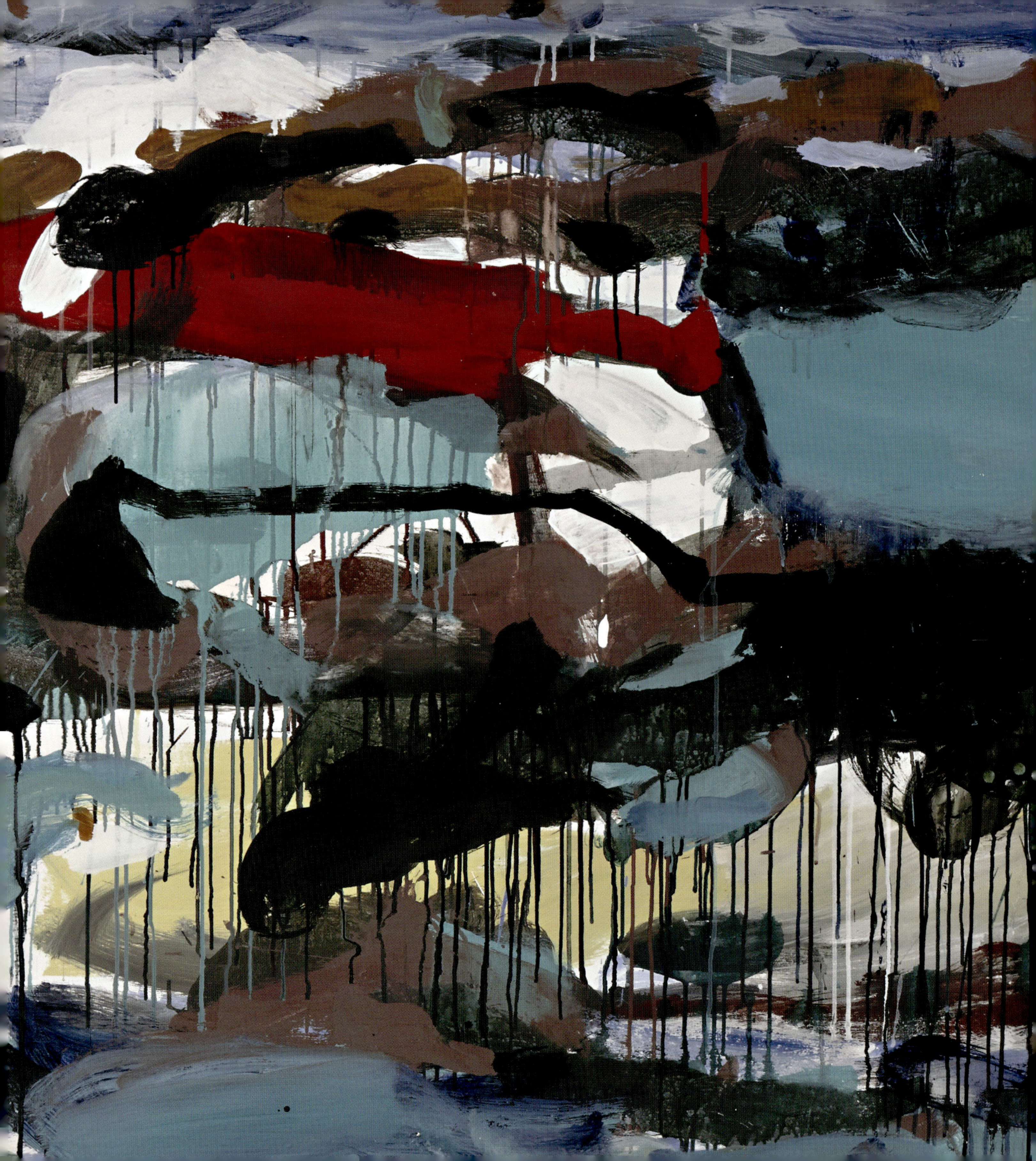

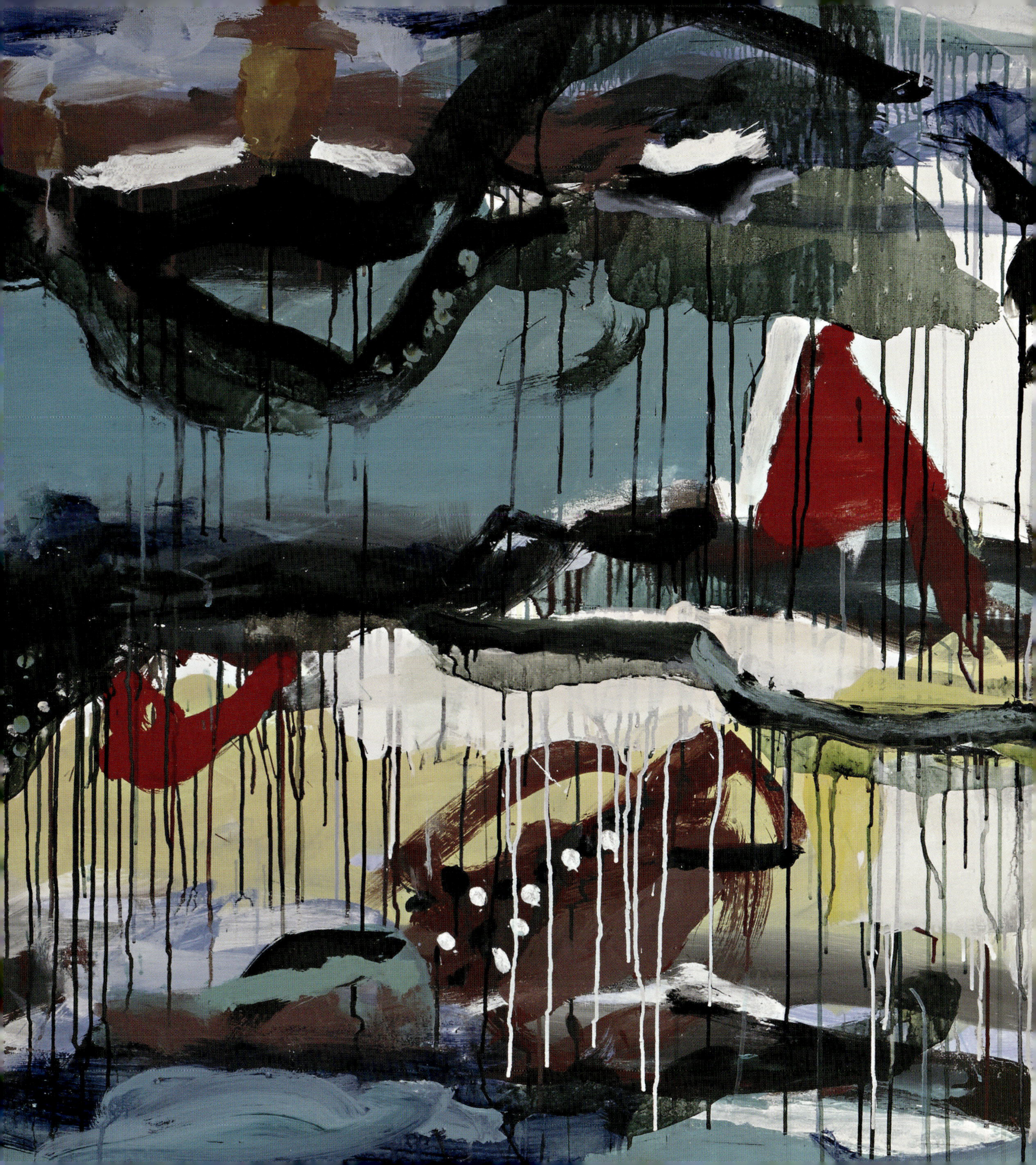

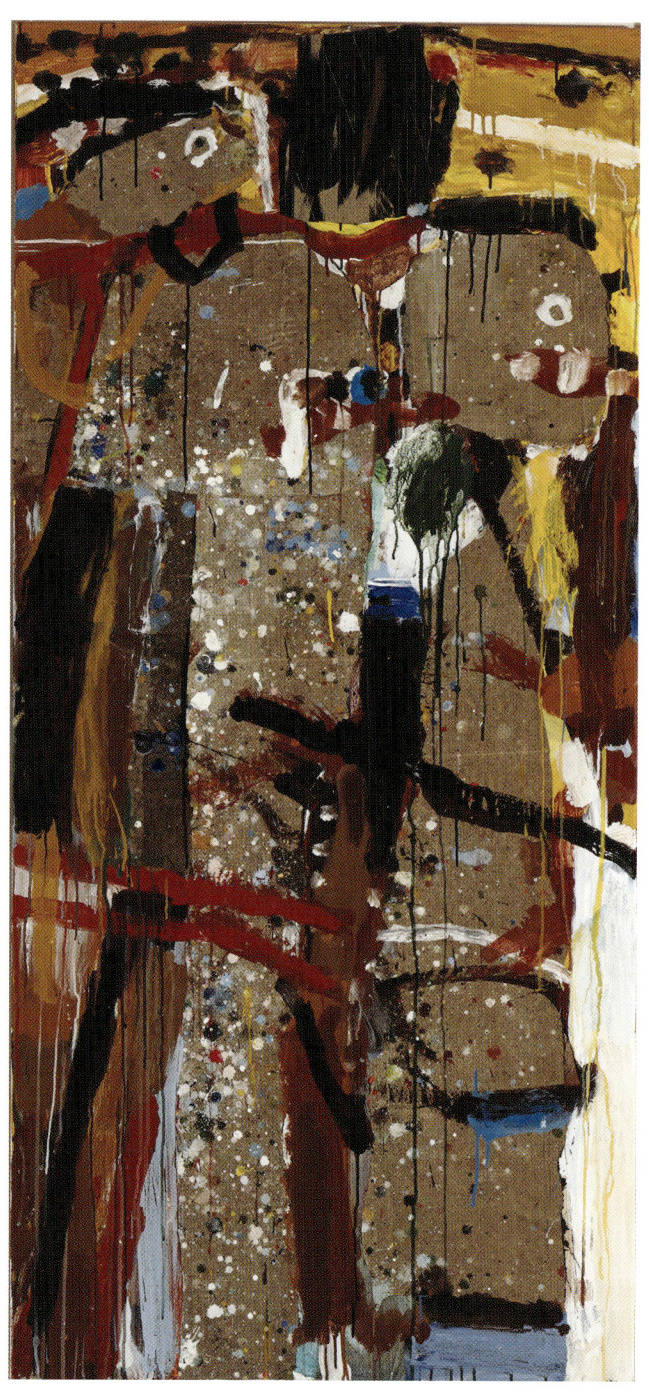

Triad 2012, acrylic and collage on linen, 183 x 83 cm. Courtesy Ann Thomson

previous page: *Sea-entrance* 2014, arylic on linen, 112 x 204 cm. Courtesy Ann Thomson

foreword

Fifty years ago, in 1965, Ann Thomson held her first solo exhibition at Watters Gallery in Sydney. It was two years ago, in 2013, that she entered her eightieth year. Five years previous to that, in 2008, one began to notice signs of change in her art – changes that could not be ascribed to the attrition of age. On the contrary: her paintings and drawings were growing conspicuously stronger, wilder and freer. To all intents and purposes, they had begun to grow younger.

"Youthfulness in painting is slowly achieved," wrote Jean Bazaine, a French artist born in 1904 who continued to paint well into his nineties. "It is granted as a reward to the old-timers who merit it. You need to drink long and deeply of the milk of life before it starts to go to your head."

How true this is in Ann Thomson's case. In a monograph about her work published in 2012, there is a photograph of an adolescent Ann leaping down the side of a sand-dune. Physical exuberance is innate to her, and it is expressed more strongly than ever in her recent work. Her feeling for pulse and rhythm, for irrepressible physical energies projected into space, imbues her pictorial conceptions with a great vivacity. Paintings such as *Orion* 2014 and *Water poised above water* 2014, for instance, could be read as sequences of dance-steps at the same time as evoking embryonic landscapes or seascapes. Another keynote of her recent paintings is their feeling of spaciousness, flow and respiration – as if every part of a work is breathing as one, as if the whole thing was resumed in a single breath.

"The painter is born old," Jean Bazaine wrote in 1973, and his meditations written late in life have attracted some noteworthy commentaries – in particular those of Valérie Zuchuat, who wrote a gloss on this statement:

> The painter is old not only because of his or her memories, but above all because of rules followed and lessons learnt, all the forms of defence – the ultimate in education – erected against the fear of losing oneself in the throes of creation…Gradually liberated from these constraints, the painter allows what he [Bazaine] calls the "genius of childhood" to emerge. What is this genius? Desire? An innate disposition to create? An instinctive openness to the world? A talent one doesn't yet know? No doubt it is something of all of these at once.

That seems to explain something important about the works in this exhibition. We at the Drill Hall Gallery are conscious of our privilege in presenting a survey of Ann Thomson's paintings, drawings and collages from the last seven years. These have been years of wonder, not only measured by the high standards Ann Thomson has always set herself – they should be years of wonder to us all.

Terence Maloon
Director Drill Hall Gallery

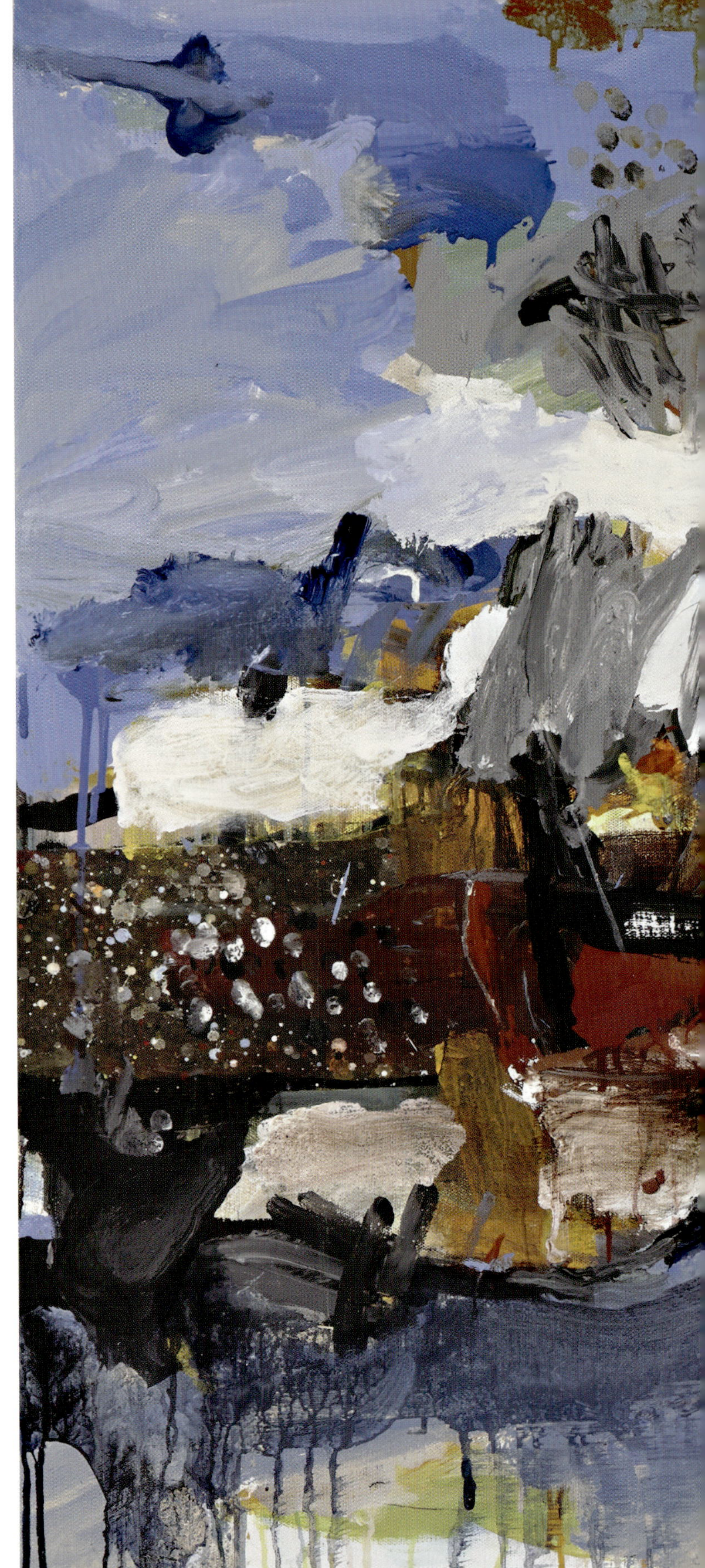

Breakwater 2014, acrylic and collage on linen, 91 × 122 cm.
Courtesy Ann Thomson

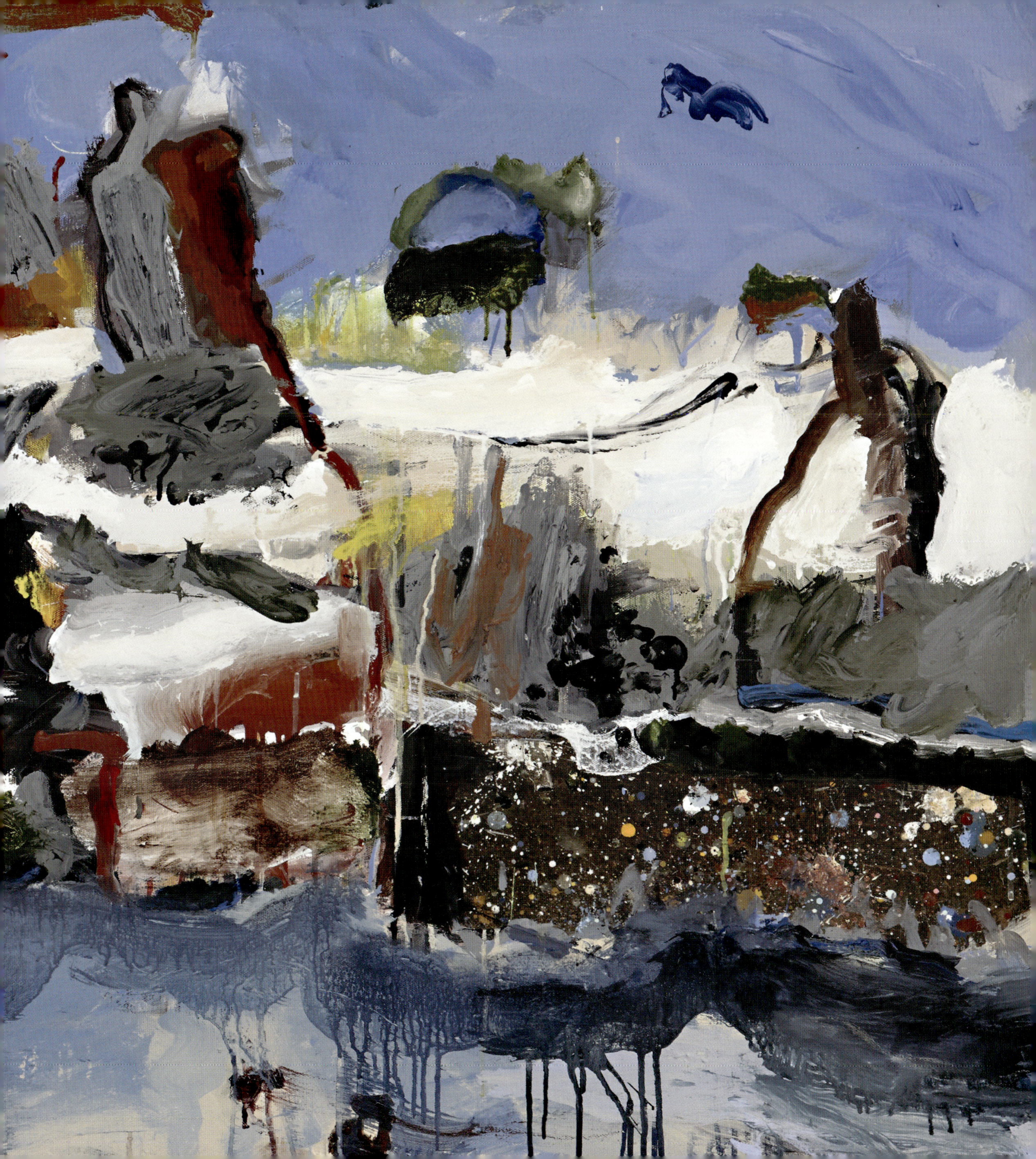

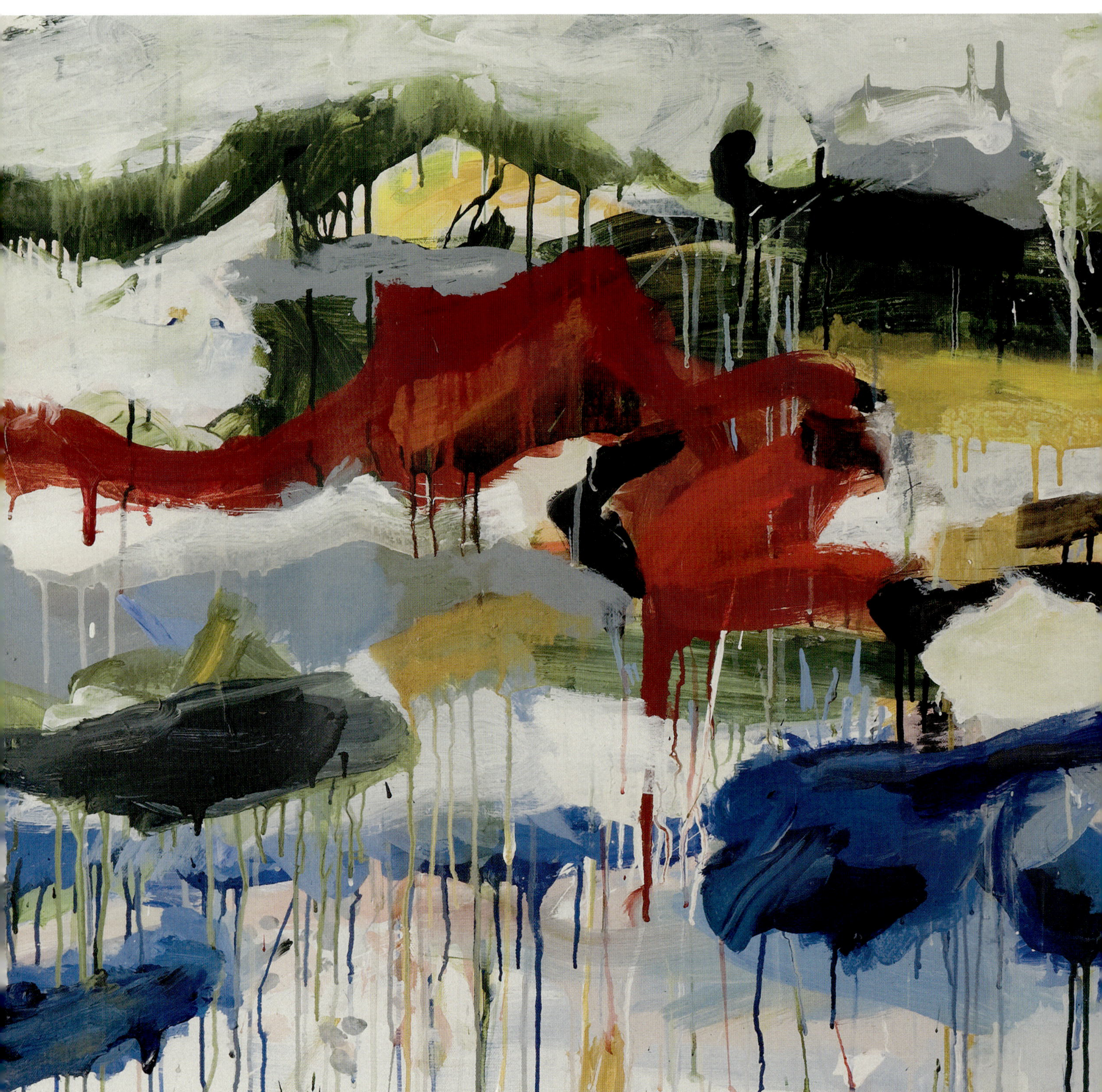

Stave 2011, acrylic on linen, 82 × 166 cm. Private collection, Sydney

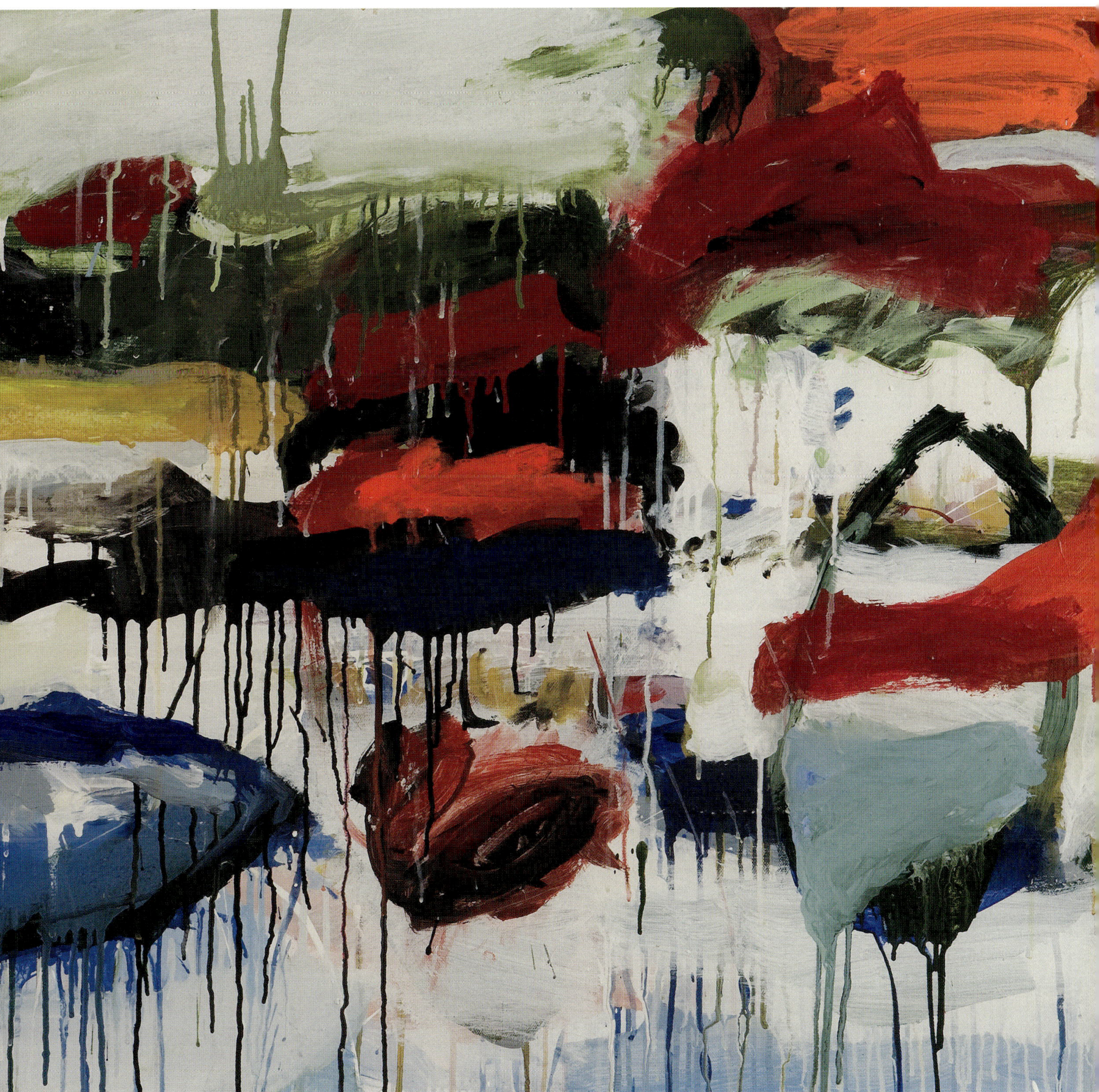

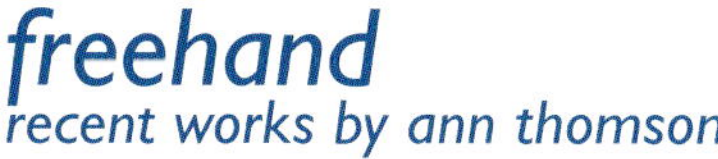

freehand
recent works by ann thomson

> "They have searched for an art whose language moves us yet is beyond distinct representation, an art that no longer imitates anything, but is content to evoke, being only allusion, suggestion, symbol…" – Louis Gillet[1]

In April 1948, eight years before the teenaged Ann Thomson began studying painting with Jon Molvig in Brisbane, the American art critic Clement Greenberg published an article whose contents were amazingly prescient of concerns that preoccupied painters during the latter half of the twentieth century. Of course, Thomson's home town of Brisbane and the burgeoning Manhattan art scene were worlds apart – completely out of synch in 1948 – and so the contentions of Greenberg's article would probably have struck locals as outlandish and inexplicable, had any of them chanced to read it.

Even the title of the article was provocative, especially in an Australian context: "The Crisis of the Easel Picture." One can imagine the consternation and fury it would have unleashed if any respected Australian artist, or any person in authority, had taken it at face value at the time. Easel painting and all of its conventional attributes – figuration, pictorial illusion, a tightly controlled, reined-in technique, and picturesqueness in general – were and always had been the stock in trade of Australian art, prescribed by the market, by the museum world and by art education. The assumption that easel-painting might require re-thinking, let alone that it could be surpassed or circumvented in some way, would have struck people as foolhardy, illogical and downright dangerous.

When Greenberg's essay was anthologised thirteen years later in his book *Art and Culture* (by which time Ann Thomson was a student at the National Art School in Sydney), its subversive potential remained fantastic, its implications shattering.[2]

With the benefit of hindsight, we can now read it as a straightforward plug for Jackson Pollock and other abstract-expressionist painters who were working in New York at the time. Of course it was those painters – not Greenberg, nor any art critic or theorist – who brought about the crisis of the easel picture. The painters in question had their precursors (some of whom Greenberg acknowledged in his article) and their contemporaries in Europe (likewise), all of whom shared a general sense of dissatisfaction: a feeling of being hamstrung and frustrated by the littleness, the confinement, the craftiness and air of unreality of the easel-painting tradition. They shared the need to break out of it.

When Matisse was asked in a 1952 interview whether he thought easel painting had much of a future, he replied:

> I think that one day easel painting will no longer exist because of changing customs. There will be mural painting. Colours win you over more and more. A certain blue enters your soul. A certain red has an effect on your blood pressure. A certain colour tones you up. It's the concentration of timbres. A new era is opening.[3]

Clearly, Ann Thomson's art was (and is) part of this new era. Yet what are the factors that make the era distinct from the previous one? What makes this kind of painting significantly new? As Matisse's statement clearly implies, there was a desire for greater immediacy, greater vividness and greater concreteness felt by many artists. They sought a more intense, visceral engagement with the actuality, with the *stuff* of their art, and the reorientation of their priorities affected viewers as well.

By and large, easel paintings are imaginary worlds that appeal to the mind's eye. The new art that Greenberg (and Matisse, Pollock, de Kooning, etc) envisaged was an art that involved the whole body. It had to be read (so to speak) with, against, in relation to the body. Mind and body were presumed to be one and the same thing. In contrast, the viewer of easel paintings was implicitly disembodied – he or she was a point in space, a point-of-view, immobile, scaleless, split-off from the fictitious world on the opposite side of the picture-frame.

For those ready to make the break, the conventions of easel painting had to be overturned in order to intensify a painting's physical charge – whether this resided in a "concentration of timbres" (as Matisse put it), or in the revelation of the bones, nerves and sinews of the painting's compositional structure (as Pollock, de Kooning and, later, Ann Thomson proposed), or in a new poetics of surface and scale, where abstractness (non-referentiality, truth-to-materials) was axiomatic. These changes in the conventions of painting can be explained on philosophical, religious and ideological grounds as well. If easel painting had been a privileged vehicle for such a long time, one reason was that its conventions corresponded to ideas of the self and of the objective world that had become entrenched in common sense. These ideas were mooted by Brunelleschi and others in the fifteenth century, and were theorized by Descartes in the seventeenth century and by Newton in the eighteenth; over the centuries they had become commonplace.

Yet one of the long-term "projects" of the modern age has been to release the human body from its Cartesian/Newtonian definition, to release it from its bourgeois, puritanical and Judeo-Christian inhibitions, to free it from servitude to purely practical aims, and to reclaim the integrality of body and soul.[4] Art, of course, has had its role in this process.

For our purposes it is sufficient to note that "the crisis of the easel picture" occurred at the juncture when Ann Thomson came to maturity, when she entered the history of Australian art, and when her art's identity was definitively shaped. And for its on-the-spot diagnosis of the sea-change happening in painting in the middle of the twentieth century, Greenberg's testimony remains invaluable – both for what it says and what it doesn't, and notwithstanding the extreme differences in circumstance separating the Macquarie Galleries in Sydney (where the ground-breaking exhibition, *Direction 1*, took place in 1956) and Tenth Street in New York, whose galleries, by the time *Direction 1* was held, already teemed with a super-abundance of paintings by abstract-expressionist epigones of de Kooning and Franz Kline, much to Greenberg's disapproval: he was just about ready to jettison the lot of them as early as 1955, it would seem![5]

Greenberg's essay appeared in two forms – the original 1948 version and a revised version published in 1961. In the 1948 version he described the earliest inklings of a crisis of easel painting occurring in the 1880s, in works by Monet and Pissarro which had begun to "reduce the picture to a relatively undifferentiated surface." The accentuated materiality of their painting and their "democratic" evenness of treatment of foregrounds and backgrounds and solids and voids were antithetical to the conventions of easel-painting – to conventions that had pertained up till that time.

Bearing these insights in mind we can measure the depth and reach of the Impressionists' influence on modern art, since similar features prevail to this day in Ann Thomson's works, and are conspicuous in the paintings of her teachers and immediate forerunners, namely: Jon Molvig, Godfrey Miller, John Passmore and Ian Fairweather. The kind of modern painting that they proposed was *dense*, and Miller, Passmore and Fairweather shared the tendency of certain American abstract-expressionists to "weave the work of art into a tight mesh whose principle of formal unity is contained and recapitulated in every thread, so that we find the essence of the whole work in every one of its parts." [6]

When Greenberg revised his 1948 essay for re-publication in 1961, he made a few changes which reflected the benefit of hindsight: the clogging-up of illusionistic space and the incipient all-overness of classic Impressionist paintings no longer seemed so vitally important to him. More than any other contender, it was Monet's late waterlily paintings which now appeared to have most "threatened the easel-picture convention, and […] twenty years after [his] death, become the point of departure for a new tendency in painting."[7]

Monet's late works ushered in the *big picture*: their panoramic scale was prophetic of the formats of abstract expressionism, as was the explicitness of Monet's handwriting – the eruptive flurries, the long ribbony trails, the scribbles and scatterings that magically joined up, merging and melding into a continuum. In the classic Impressionist paintings of the 1880s, congested surfaces and clogged-up aerial perspective came to seem intolerably claustrophobic to some practitioners, and so did the Impressionists' method of applying colour in repetitive staccato dabs. Monet's need to break out of the easel-painting format and to develop an expansive gestural language was so far ahead of its time that his late waterlily paintings still

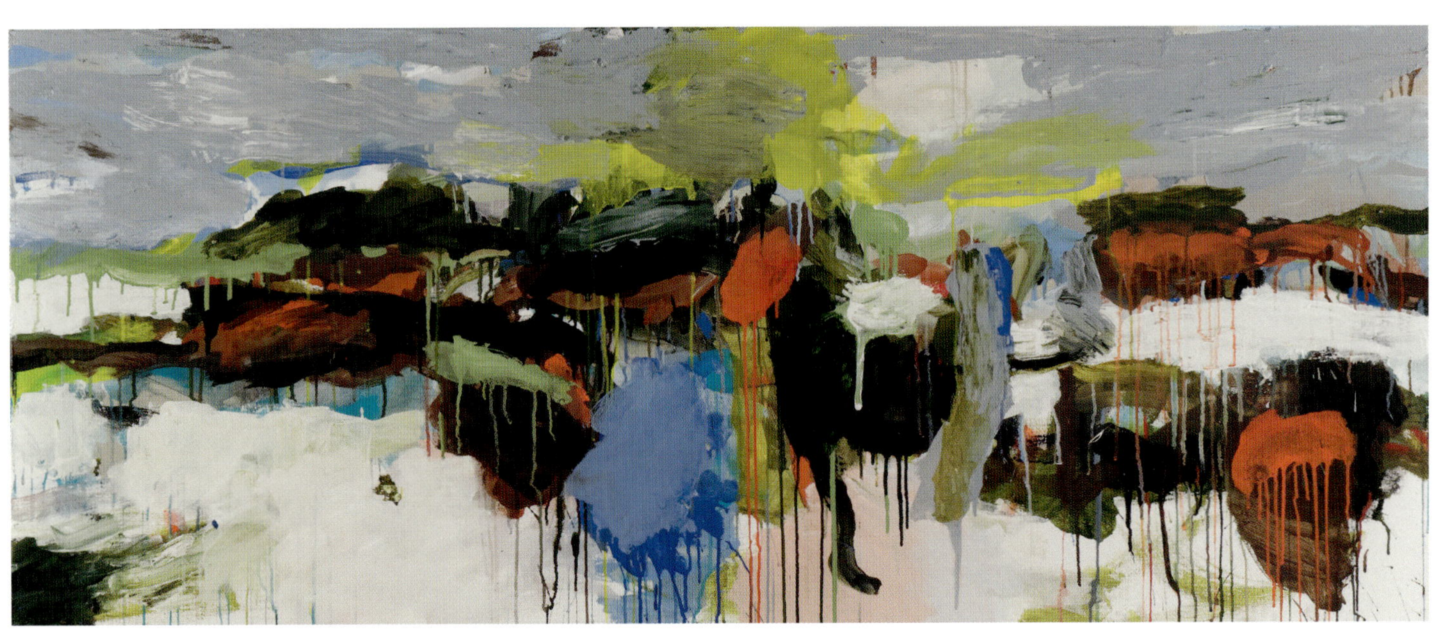

Dawn 2011, acrylic on linen, 82 × 190 cm. Private collection, Sydney

opposite: *Argentine* 2014, acrylic on linen, 100 × 100 cm. Courtesy Ann Thomson and Olsen Irwin Gallery, Sydney

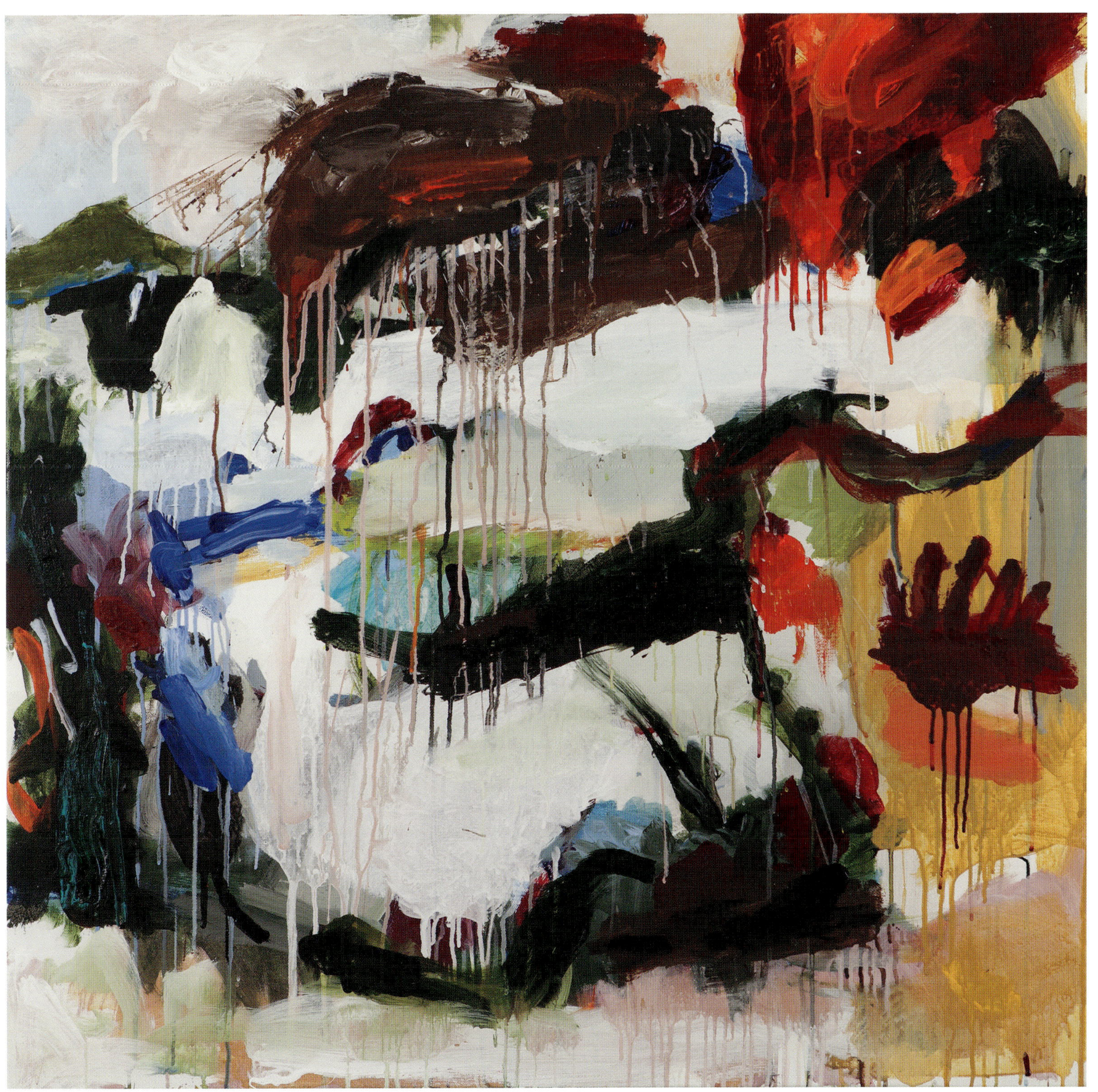

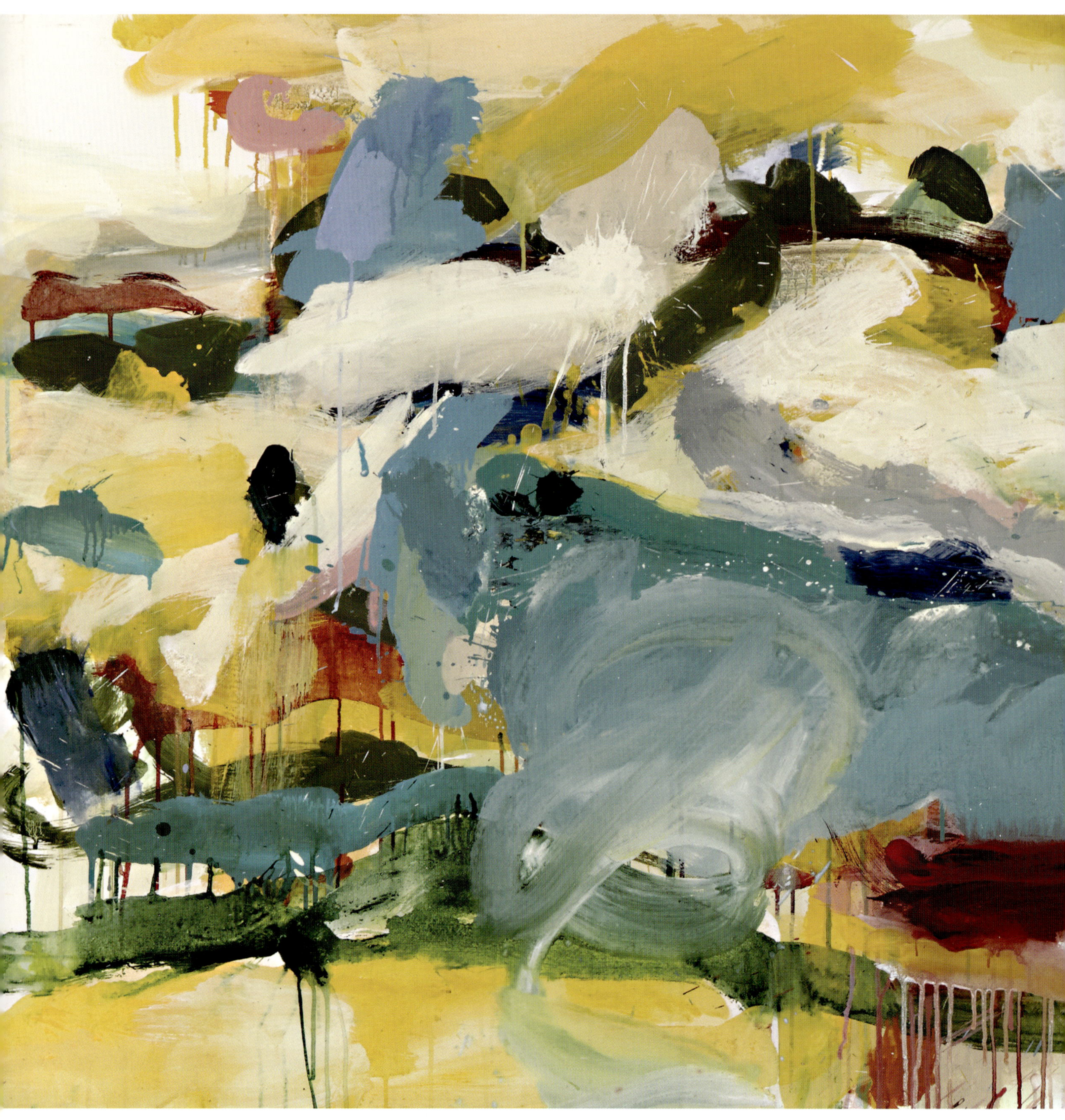

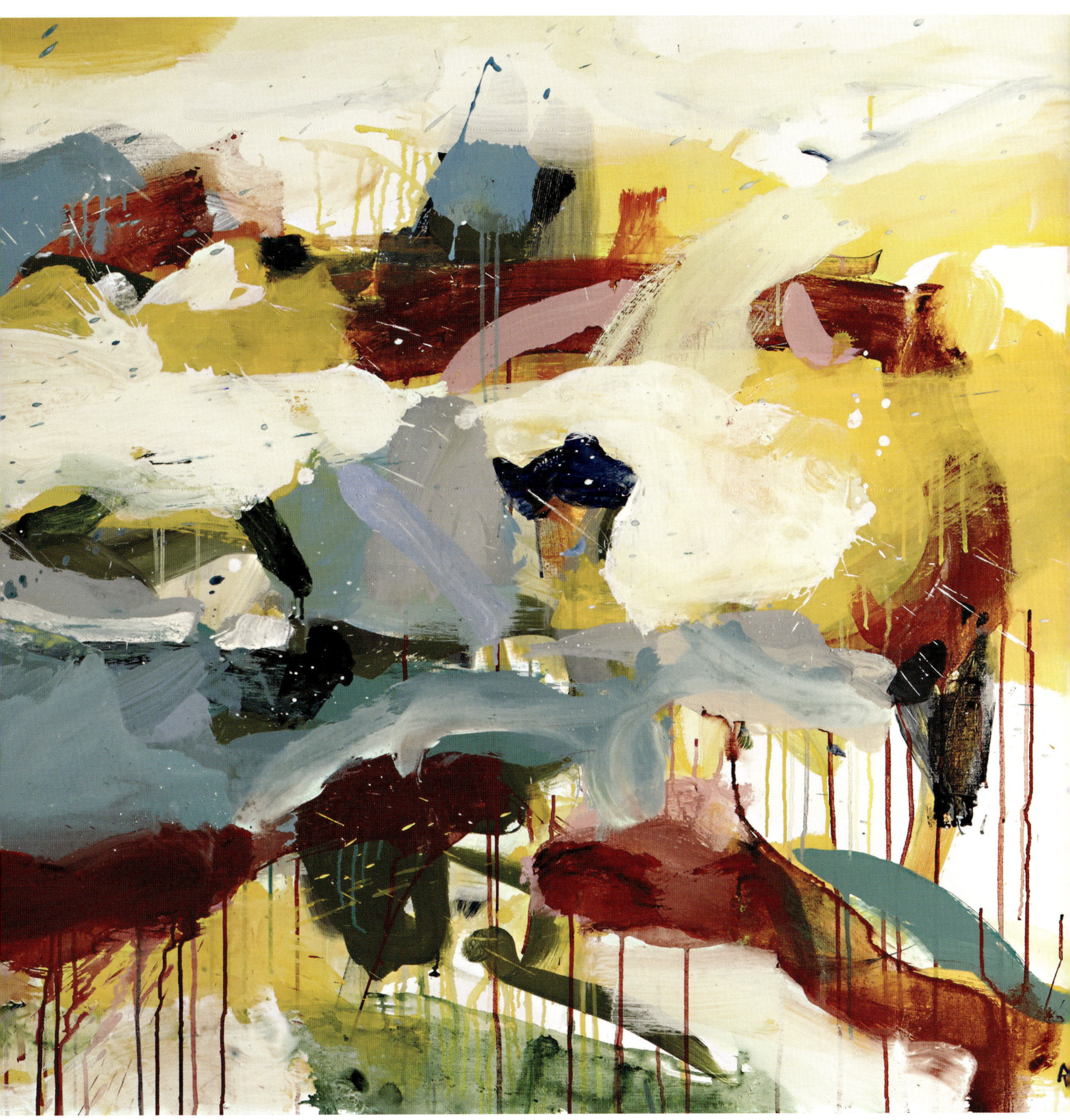

seemed completely up-to-date and relevant some thirty, forty years after his death. The lesson to be derived from his (and Pollock's) breakthrough was that, when painting becomes so dense and opaque, it needs to get bigger and alter its relation to the body and the body's movements. (In a review published in 1948, Greenberg advised Arshile Gorky that he "should rely more on the movement of his whole arm than on that of his wrist or elbow alone.")[8]

The *big picture* in America was introduced principally by Pollock (whom de Kooning credited with having "broken the ice") and became the specialty of very individual painters such as Barnett Newman and Mark Rothko (who were the antipodes of Pollock and de Kooning in some respects). In Australia, a parallel "crisis of the easel picture" was effected by John Olsen, Tony Tuckson and Peter Upward, and their paintings of the late 1950s and early 1960s really do "sing the body electric." Bernard Smith credited Olsen with bringing "a new energy and character to Sydney painting," [9] a lesson that was not lost on Ann Thomson who was a student of Olsen's at the National Art School during his *Wunderjahre* of 1960-62.[10] The revelation of Tuckson's achievement came belatedly to everyone, yet it was no less crucial: Tuckson had been a non-exhibiting, "underground" painter between 1953 and 1970, but his late works are outstanding because of their incandescent physicality – a fact that Ann Thomson was well able to appreciate.[11]

You can still detect a reminiscence of Monet's waterlilies in Thomson's painting *Stave* (pp 10 -11), which shares a general orientation to the horizontal, even if Thomson's language of painting is much more discontinuous and abrupt than Monet's, and there is no longer any safety-net of tonalism nor any obvious basis in "harmony."[12] Every element, every shape in Thomson's painting derives its character from the gauge of her brush. Patches of blues, reds, yellow ochre, green and black alternate with patches of white and shades of off-white, yet, while there is a constant temptation to read the whites as *background,* they aren't permitted to disengage and recede: there is no background in the painting, strictly speaking.

In *Stave*, the family of whites occupy a more or less equal ratio to the aggregates of intense colour, and they assert an equivalent presence, solidifying, jostling and interpenetrating with the colours, yet they do not do this too insistently: the subtlety and skill of Thomson's art consists of obtaining the maximum integration of parts while avoiding gridlock. The relationship between colour and ostensible non-colour remains tenuous enough to admit the play of spatial illusion and give free rein to the suggestion of light and air.

Fringes of dribbles are a reminder of the law of gravity, but Thomson's brushmarks consistently resist and defy gravity. As with Monet's waterlilies, hers is a "floating world"; the dribbling trails are foils that accentuate the brushmarks' venturesome, airborne character.[13] Through their clustering and overlapping, and through the spatial suggestions arising from relationships of colour and tone, tracks of the brush are transformed into a series of planes that shuffle into a precisely conceived aerial perspective (or, alternately, into several variants of perspective), yet the spatial illusion – vivid and compelling though it is – is fleeting and reversible.

previous page: *Orion* 2014, acrylic on linen, 102 cm x 200 cm Courtesy Ann Thomson and Olsen Irwin Gallery, Sydney

A flotsam of waterlilies; jetsam on a sea shore; a riverbank, sky, a rural landscape; fruits, a still-life on a shelf or table top; the light of nature; some aspect of the Australian continent; the mental trace of an experience past, present or future; an atmosphere; a sense of "being there" – now you think you see and feel it, now you don't. This imagery is deliberately triggered, but it is programmed to unravel and mutate. It is an imagery of the slipping glimpse – an imagery not so much ephemeral as continuously regenerating in front of our eyes. The syntax of the painting remains firm, yet what we read into it proves highly unstable. Indeed, what arises in the mind's eye is a fugue of slipping glimpses – "images that yet fresh images beget" (as Yeats put it); and the sheer subjectivity of the experience corresponds to what another poet, Gerard Manley Hopkins, called *inscape* and *instress*: in general, Thomson's paintings are very much *inscapes*.[14]

To grasp the subtlety of her visual language, it is useful to compare Thomson's *Stave* to another work painted close to it in time, featuring a similar palette and having an identical format. Thomson aimed for each colour in *Stave* to strike a clear note, finding intervals between the colours that would bring out the purity and the separateness of every register. But something quite different happens in *Dawn* (p16): the centre of gravity in the composition has shifted to the middle of the canvas, and a concussion of shards of colour has resulted in some fraying and bleeding which Thomson has cannily exploited, using the nuances of shot colour and tinges that have crept into the whites to conjure up a whole atmospherics. The painting's proclivity to mother-of-pearl and evocation of a landscape-like depth of field is given even more leeway in *Argentine* (p17) – yet, despite the obvious differences between these three paintings, there is no sense of the artist changing her approach and (for example) lingering unduly over lovely glimmering effects or deciding at some point to pursue an idea of *landscape*. At this time in her life, Thomson's language of painting rarely falters in its brisk efficiency and lucidity of purpose. Her idiom is characteristically taut, succinct and pacey; she has refined and personalized her language to a remarkable degree, developing a completely unshowy virtuosity. "Painting is composition," she will repeat – lest we forget it. That we are able to judge the adequacy and appropriateness of her brushmarks as *language* is due to the way they function as parts of a whole.

Every brushmark in Thomson's paintings links up with other brushmarks and with the developing image as a whole. This calls to mind Clement Greenberg's characterization of certain modern paintings where "the essence of the whole work is in every one of its parts": the essential element of Thomson's paintings is a kind of hyphen. The French word for "hyphen," *trait d'union*, means: a line that unites, a line that links. For Thomson, the art of composition involves the multiplication of such linkages, sowing the maximum interconnectedness in bringing an image together. ("The whole thing is to put in as much rapport as possible," Cézanne explained.)

The exhibition that is generally credited with having launched abstract expressionism in Australia, *Direction I,* was greeted with a howling opposition that continued unabated for many years. A counter-attack was mounted by Bernard Smith in Melbourne in 1959, with

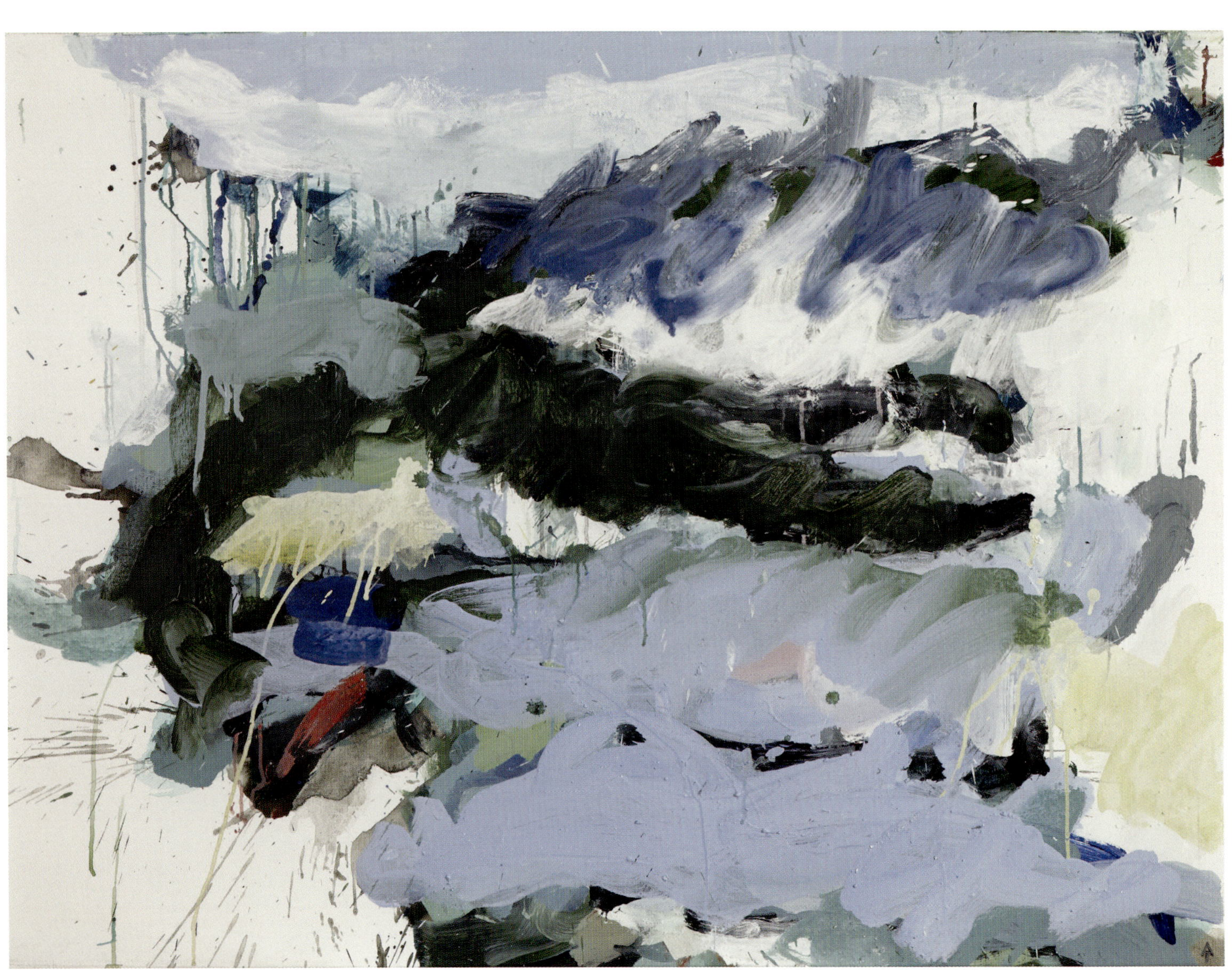

 Cloudburst 2014, acrylic on linen, 93 x 121 cm. Courtesy Ann Thomson and Olsen Irwin Gallery, Sydney

an exhibition of figurative painters who called themselves *The Antipodeans*. Their manifesto targeted "Tachistes, Action Painters, Geometric Abstractionists, Abstract Expressionists" whose paintings (sight unseen) were said not to be "sufficient for our time." The confusing mish-mash of names that Smith cited in the Antipodean manifesto implied that the artists in Europe and America affiliated with these movements were a rabble of half-baked opportunists and empty-headed trendies. It was suggested that, at very least, such abstract drivel could be quarantined to Sydney. In fact, the Antipodeans regarded abstract expressionism as a *Sydney* phenomenon, and claimed that it was due to the dereliction of the Sydney critics that this kind of art had been permitted to take root on Australian soil.

It is sobering to read the mud-slinging fifty years on, since so much of it still sounds very familiar. It was a knee-jerk response, no doubt – compounded not just of provincialism and curmudgeonliness, but also the self-justification of artists who felt that they were under-rewarded and under-recognized, resentful of any attention being taken away from them. Whenever the status quo feels threatened in this way, the threat is usually ascribed to a publicity stunt, a marketing exercise or a plot to brain-wash the public. The perpetrators are said to be copycats of artistic fashions overseas (with those fashions already obsolete and entirely discredited before they have reached Australian shores). The artists are suspected of being the agents of American imperialism. The kind of art they propose is alien to the great Australian tradition. They are promoting the de-skilling of artists and the mystification and dumbing-down of the art audience. Their art's newness and strangeness are *academic* and *passé* even before it has had time to reveal its possibilities.

The reception of *so-called* abstract expressionism in Australia happened in just this way – "so-called abstract expressionism", because the paintings in *Direction I* would, most likely, not be recognised as such by anyone today. The dominant influences – far from being the wild men of New York – were School of Paris artists like Estève, Manessier and Vieira da Silva, whose works had been seen in Sydney a couple of years earlier in an exhibition entitled *French Painting Today* at the Art Gallery of New South Wales – and also André Bazaine (not included in the exhibition, but evidently known through reproductions of his paintings in art magazines.) It is indicative of how volatile and paranoid the art world was at the time, that *Direction I* was felt to rock its foundations – foundations that were based upon picturesqueness, storytelling, symbolism, a nationalistic, white-fellow ideology and, of course, the marketability of easel paintings.

It is a striking fact that Ann Thomson's work never succumbed to the dichotomies that the opponents of *Direction I* were so eager to perpetuate: between abstract and figurative; modernism and tradition; Europe and America; Australia and the rest – not to mention between Melbourne and Sydney. As a matter of principle, and as a function of her intelligence and sensitivity, Thomson keeps a good distance between her art and any loaded ideological situation, and never requires any solidarity and like-mindedness from her audience; as Stéphane Jacob put it, "Ann never imposes her vision: she merely suggests. It is up to the viewer to adapt and reinterpret the given scene according to his or her predilections – to each his own."[15]

Because he has experienced Australia as an itinerant Frenchman, not as a permanent resident, Stéphane Jacob doesn't share some of the complexes and inhibitions we Australians have when talking about Aboriginal and Balanda (white-fellow) art in the same breath. Jacob is able to write about the sensations he experienced while travelling through the Australian landscape and how he finds echoes of them in Ann Thomson's works, including reminiscences "both vague and precise" of Aboriginal rock paintings in northern Australia:

> My head was teeming with images gleaned from all the places I had been to in this strikingly beautiful and vast land. The intensity of the light, the strength of the colours, the magic of the early morning skies, the exquisite harmony of the last rays of the setting sun striking the silvery trunks of the eucalyptus trees… And then the waterholes with their specific chromatic harmonies; the oxidized rock; the rocks whose texture resembles a prehistoric animal's skin; the spinifex rolling over the ground; the red earth; the sandy, powdery, rocky earth… the smell of dried leaves, and then… And then there was Ann's work, which was like an invitation to the voyage.[16]

This description seems to me spot-on. Shunning one-sidedness and resisting any too-definite readings of her imagery, Ann Thomson pursues a policy of inclusiveness that keeps a utopian dream alive in her art. In the suspended, dream-like atmospheres that her paintings evoke, determinations of cultural difference, race and gender (for example) lose any authoritative, limiting hold they may have over our imaginations. And as a veteran swimmer, the undersea world holds sway over her imagery nearly as tenaciously as the landscapes of dry land: submarine evocations can be discerned in recent works such as *Utopia* 2011 and *Sea-entrance* 2014.

One of the momentous repercussions brought about by the crisis of the easel picture in Australia was that, during the early 1970s, some of the ritual practices of Aboriginal people of Central Australia were able to cross the divide, and they became the basis of a new kind of Western Desert painting. By bringing together their traditional body-painting designs and the mental maps of their dreaming sites and songlines, Aboriginal painters could conflate *body* and *landscape* imagery – which, as we have seen, is Ann Thomson's predilection as well.[17]

Being extremely receptive to the poetic qualities and understanding the relativism of Ann Thomson's work, Stéphane Jacob is led by those qualities to speculate about how individual works might appear if seen from other angles – reoriented to the floor, looked at from another side. And once again he touches on an important insight, for the flexibility and convergence of several points of view is characteristic of Thomson's approach, and has been a feature of her work virtually from the start of her career. In fact Stéphane Jacob's remark returns us to some of Thomson's 1970s works featuring flying machines.

Windy Straits 2014, acrylic on linen, 122 x 122 cm. Courtesy Ann Thomson and Olsen Irwin Gallery, Sydney

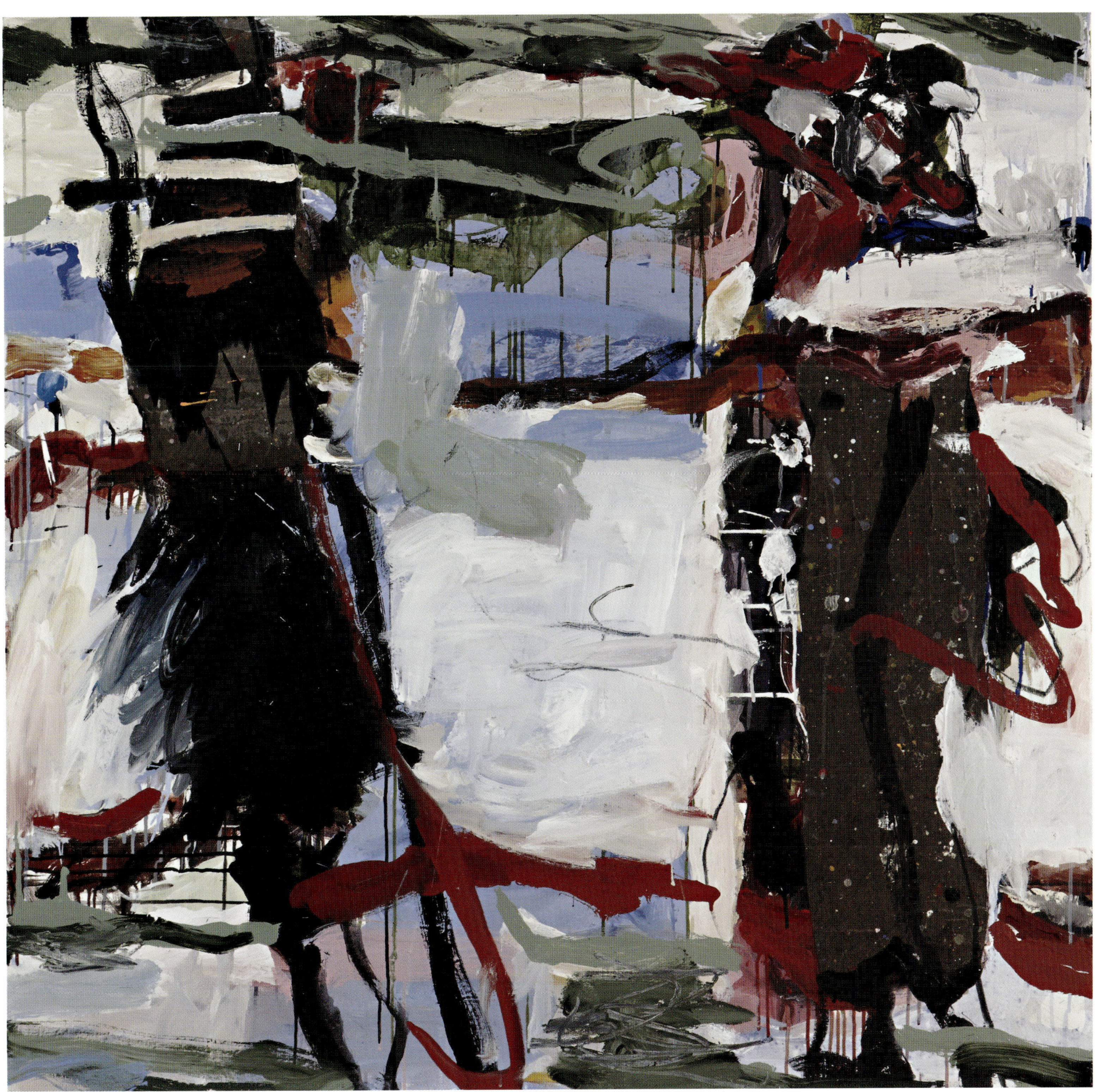

Like the sailing vessels whose rigging would haunt her works during the 1980s, the flying-machine motif in her earlier paintings extended an "invitation to the voyage." On the face of it, the motif must have been useful in making the abstractness of these paintings less strange and off-putting to people who would normally baulk at "modern art," passing off the paintings as ventures into uncharted space, into fantasy lands, into environments where the laws of nature applied differently. Since early days, Thomson has claimed liberties which she never renounced, foremost of which are: non-naturalistic space and a non-naturalistic palette. For a while her colour was sweet and flowery, possibly influenced by the Queensland-resident painter, Sam Fullbrook (1922-2004). But, given that her impetuous brushwork was seriously committed to compositional aims and tended to shirk the menial tasks of describing and detailing, those "magnificent men in their flying machines" were little more than go-betweens and alibis, with the flimsiness of their Heath-Robinson vehicles accentuated by the tentative, whimsical way they were painted and drawn. Her over-riding interest was in the possible worlds that *painting itself* could reveal to an intrepidly creative spirit, not the wry alter-egos purporting to be explorers and discoverers of a never-never land.

Nonetheless, whether through foreknowledge or inspired intuition, the flying machines in Thomson's paintings were indeed harbingers of abstraction – at least they had been so during the heyday of Blériot and the Wright brothers, which was also the epoch of Picasso and Braque (who nicknamed each other "Orville" and "Wilbur" after the Wright brothers), and Robert and Sonia Delaunay (whose early abstract paintings were obsessed with aeroplanes, spinning propellers, and views from on high), and Malevich and Tatlin (both of them flight-fantasists and cosmonauts before their time; Malevich even proclaimed himself to be the President of Space.)[18] These pioneers of abstract art had all been affected in a profound way by the conquest of the air.

The creative liberties they took with aerial perspective and their predilection for a totalizing, bird's eye, "macro" view could be justified by analogy with the views obtained from the top of the Eiffel Tower or from aeroplanes, Roland Barthes has explained. The Eiffel Tower "corresponds to a new sensibility of vision," he wrote. As opposed to being "thrust into the midst of sensation, to perceive only a kind of tidal wave of things, [...] the bird's-eye view [afforded by] the Tower and the birth of aviation permits us to transcend sensation and to see things in their structure. Hence it is the advent of a new perception, of an intellectualist mode."[19]

Painting – abstract expressionist painting – is a way of conjuring with the possible: that is what attracted Ann Thomson to it initially, and sustained her commitment to it for approximately five decades. Yet what do we mean by "abstract expressionist painting"? Is it a style? An art movement? An American influence? A fad of the 1950s? Abstract expressionism is a misnomer in her case, surely: her work is not, and never has been consistently or dogmatically abstract. She has never assumed that abstraction and representation are mutually exclusive terms. Likewise, her paintings and drawings could not strictly speaking be termed expressionist, given that the expression of feelings, moods, etc. is never a conscious aim of hers, and anything that smacks of rhetoric, or of a theatricalization of the self is abhorrent to her. Likewise, the strategies that are usually associated with an expressionist idiom – wilful uglification and distortion and an antagonistic treatment of media – these are alien to her mentality. Her main focus is on bringing out the latent qualities of the material at hand and attending to the evolving formal relationships in a work. "*Painting is composition,*" she says – to which she might add: "Painting is a language."

Clement Greenberg was much mistaken when, in 1955 or thereabouts, he was persuaded that "the expressive possibilities of abstract painterly appearance [...] had been exhausted for the time being. Painterly Abstraction had turned by and large into an assortment of ready-made effects."[20]

Equally mistaken were the Antipodeans who, like Greenberg, dismissed out of hand abstract expressionism (or as Greenberg preferred to call it, painterly abstraction) as a set of gimmicks, a fad that would be made obsolescent by yet other fads in the offing. In fact, abstract expressionism wasn't a style, nor an art movement, nor a passing fashion. The problems that arose around its naming and definition were problems of recognising what it was, what its potentials were, and what, with the passage of time, it turned out to be: a viable and sustainable language of painting.[21]

It is a language which, given the commitment, experience and talent of an artist of Ann Thomson's calibre, grows ever stronger, deeper and subtler, and engenders its own "beautiful atmosphere of reflection" – where (to adapt one of de Kooning's most famous statements) "an artist can practice her intuition".

•

[1] Louis Gillet, *Trois variations sur Claude Monet* (1909-1927), Klincksieck, Paris, 2010, p 93.

[2] Clement Greenberg, "The Crisis of the Easel Picture" (1948), in *The Collected Essays and Criticism* (4 vols, 1986-1993), vol 2, pp 221-225; Clement Greenberg, *Art and Culture*, Beacon, 1961, pp 154-157.

[3] Henri Matisse, *Matisse on Art*, trans. Jack Flam, Phaidon, London, 1984, p 143.

[4] See for example Henri Bergson: "It must be taken into account that our body is not a mathematical point in space," he wrote, adding that the result of this premise was "a false conception of the role of space and of the nature of extension." – Henri Bergson, *Matière et mémoire* (1896), Presses Universitaires de France, 1990, pp 59-60. In the same chapter ("The Natural extension of images") is a passage that chimes in very interestingly with the character of Ann Thomson's work, conveying a similar sense of being plunged in *media res*. Bergson leads the reader to a radical proposition – that our subjective experience of the self is, as it were, an experience of self (or of the mind/body) as an image among images: "Our perception in its pure state should really be part of things. And sensation, properly speaking, far from spontaneously bursting forth from the depths of our being to launch itself, in a weakened form, into space, coincides with the modifications it necessarily undergoes in the midst of the images which influence it – which influence the particular image that each of us

calls his body." *Ibid* pp 66-67. Inadvertently Bergson puts forward a strong refutation of the "expressionist" fallacy that dogs propaganda for and against "abstract expressionism".

[5] "By 1955 at the latest the expressive possibilities of abstract painterly appearance [...] had been exhausted for the time being." – Greenberg, "The 'Crisis' of Abstract Art" (1964) in *The Collected Essays and Criticism*, vol 4, p 179.

[6] Greenberg (1948) in *The Collected Essays*, vol 2, p 224.

[7] Greenberg, "The Crisis of the Easel Picture" (revised) in *Art and Culture*, p 155.

[8] Greenberg, "Review of an Exhibition of Arshile Gorky," in *The Collected Essays*, vol 2, p 221.

[9] Bernard Smith, *Australian Painting 1788-2000*, Oxford University Press, Melbourne, 2000, p 354.

[10] Thomson referred to Olsen's painting, *Spanish Encounter*, as "clamouring with suggested drawing" – see Anna Johnson, *Ann Thomson*, Tim Olsen Editions, Sydney, 2012, p 46.

[11] Thomson was one of the participants in *Up, Down and Across*, an exhibition conceived in homage to Tony Tuckson, held at the Campbelltown City Art Gallery in 1995.

[12] The parallel with modern music is close. "Harmony" became a problematic concept in modern music, just as it did in modern painting. As Stravinsky told Robert Craft, "Nobody under thirty, and only rare antediluvians like myself over thirty, uses the word 'harmony' any more, but only 'density'." – *Stravinsky in Conversation with Robert Craft*, Penguin, Harmondsworth, 1962, p 141. See also Rosalind Krauss: "As music progressed through the nineteenth century, dissonance extended this independence [of the musical note], becoming an ever more important resource for breaking into the unity of the chord in order to emancipate its separate elements and, by differentiating them, to give each a 'voice'. Dissonance [...] laid bare a sense of the objective nature of music as pure contrast, pure opposition: tempo against tempo, pitch against pitch." – Rosalind E. Krauss, *The Picasso Papers*, Thames and Hudson, London, 1998, p 14.

[13] It is interesting to recollect in this regard William Seitz's remark that Monet ushered in the "levitationary disposition of modern painting" – although I think Tiepolo may have a claim to being the first in this lineage.

[14] "Content is a glimpse, a slipping glimpse" – a famous statement by Willem de Kooning. "Those images that yet/ Fresh images beget" – WB Yeats, "Byzantium" (1930). *Inscape* and *instress* – see WH Gardner, "Introduction" in *Gerard Manley Hopkins – A Selection of his poems and prose*, Penguin Books, Harmondsworth, 1964, pp xx-xxi.

[15] Stéphane Jacob, "Ann Thomson, The French connection," in Anna Johnson, *Ann Thomson*, Tim Olsen Editions, Sydney, 2012, p 17.

[16] Ibid.

[17] In this regard, see Paul Crowther's hypothesis that the acquisition of language by children and their imaginative rapport with imagery have their origin in a principle of reciprocity deriving from "the body's correlation with the world." – Paul Crowther, *The Language of Twentieth-Century Art, A Conceptual History*, Yale University Press, London and New Haven, 1997, p 14.

[18] Malevich as the "President of Space" – see Jean-Claude Lebensztejn, "Passage: Note on the ideology of early abstraction" in Terence Maloon (ed), *Paths to Abstraction*, Art Gallery of New South Wales, Sydney, 2010, p 46.

[19] Roland Barthes, *The Eiffel Tower and Other Mythologies*, trans. Richard Howard, Hill and Wang, New York, 1979, p 9.

[20] Greenberg, "The 'Crisis' of Abstract Art" (1964) in vol 4, p 179. See also vol 4, p 99: "Painterliness in abstract art has degenerated almost everywhere into a thing of mannered and aggressive surfaces." It is not just the dogmatic finality of judgement, but the peculiar sense of geography (revealed by the phrase "almost everywhere") that gives us pause.

[21] On the problems of naming and defining abstract expressionism, see Lawrence Alloway: "The unity of Action Painting and Abstract Expressionism was purely verbal, a problem of generalization from incomplete data." – Alloway, "Systemic Painting" (1966) in *Topics in American Art since 1945*, WW Norton and Company, New York, 1975, p 77. See also the artists' forum convened in New York in 1950, where the moderator, Robert Motherwell, proposed a couple of names for the group ("Abstract-Expressionist; Abstract Symbolist; Abstract-Objectionist"), and was countered by de Kooning: "It is disastrous to name ourselves." – "Artists' Sessions at Studio 35" (1950) in Robert Motherwell and Ad Reinhardt (eds), *Modern Artists in America*, Wittenborn Schultz, Inc., New York, 1951, p 22.

"So many beings, so many things one loves have filled the painter's life, so many skies, lands, seas have entered us."
– Jean Bazaine

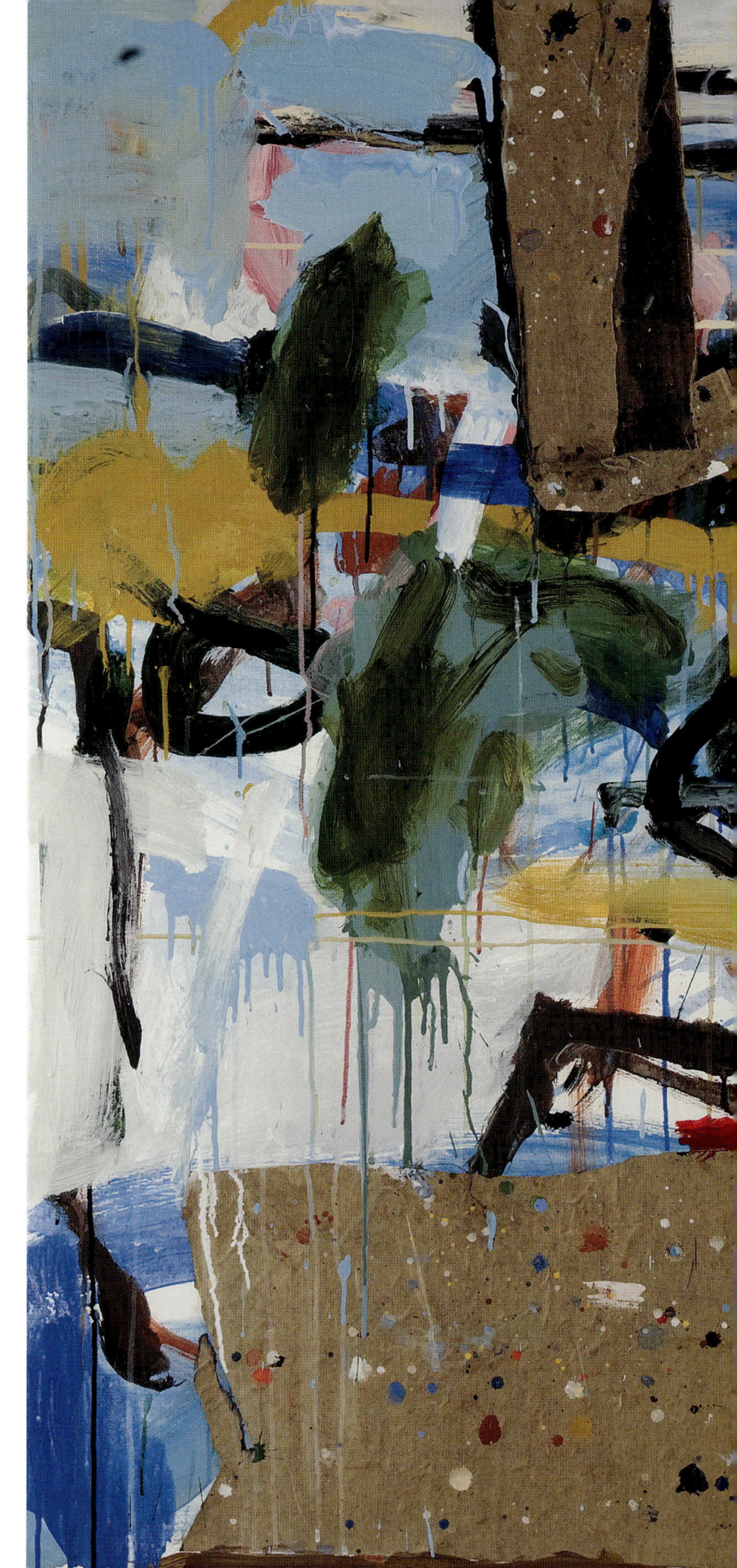

Siren 2011, acrylic and tarred paper on linen, 91cm x 122 cm.
Courtesy Ann Thomson and Olsen Irwin Gallery, Sydney

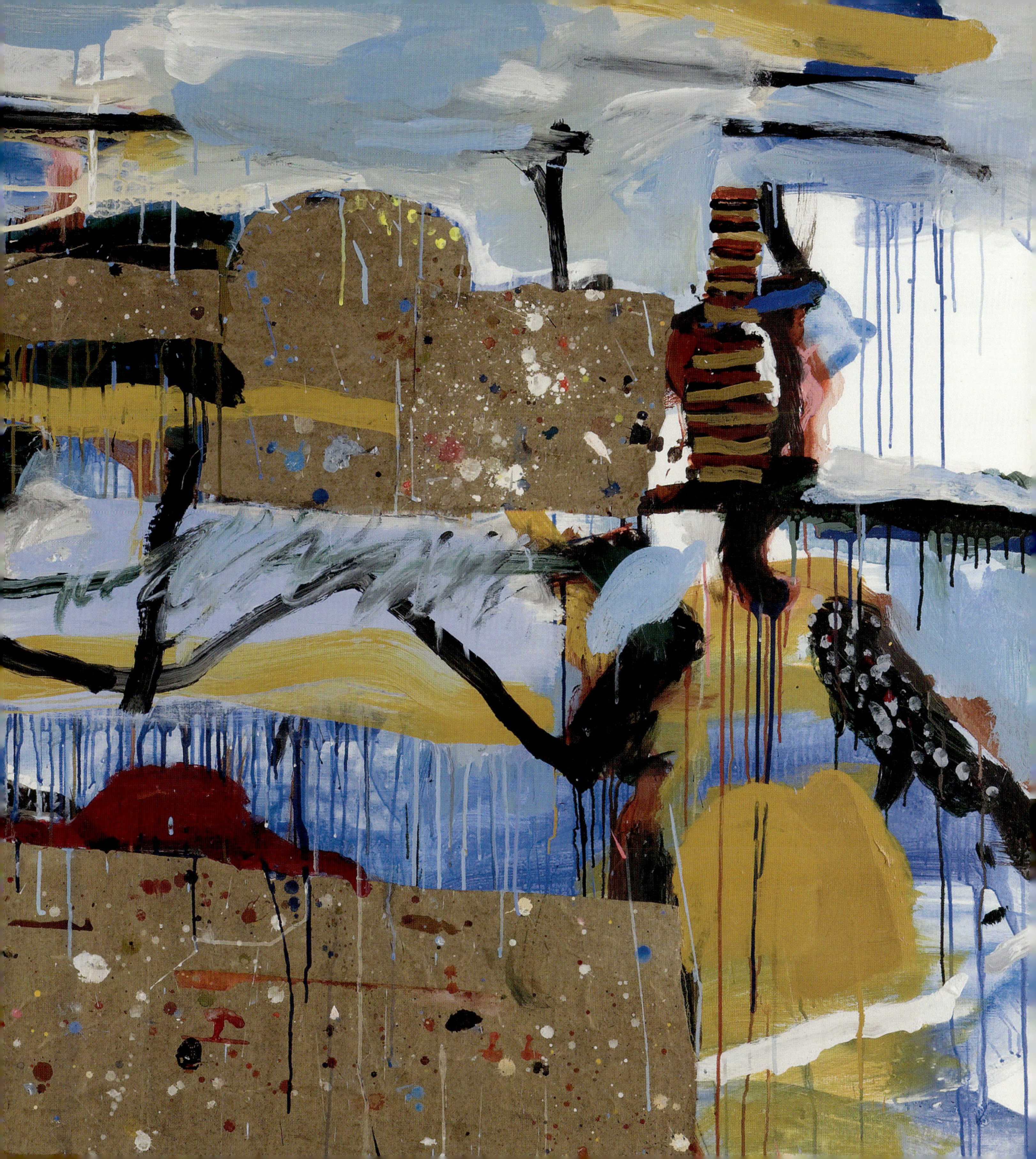

"A painter finds the true meaning of a picture only by not refusing this confused mêlée, no matter how compromised and contradictory it may appear, by accepting not to know in advance what face the painting will present, and by knowing that there are no shortcuts and deviations possible. Gradually, through the thousand facets of an elusive structure, one learns the deep, secret logic of composition."
– Jean Bazaine

Les deux magots 2011, acrylic on linen, 120 x 92 cm. Collection: Anne Deveson AO

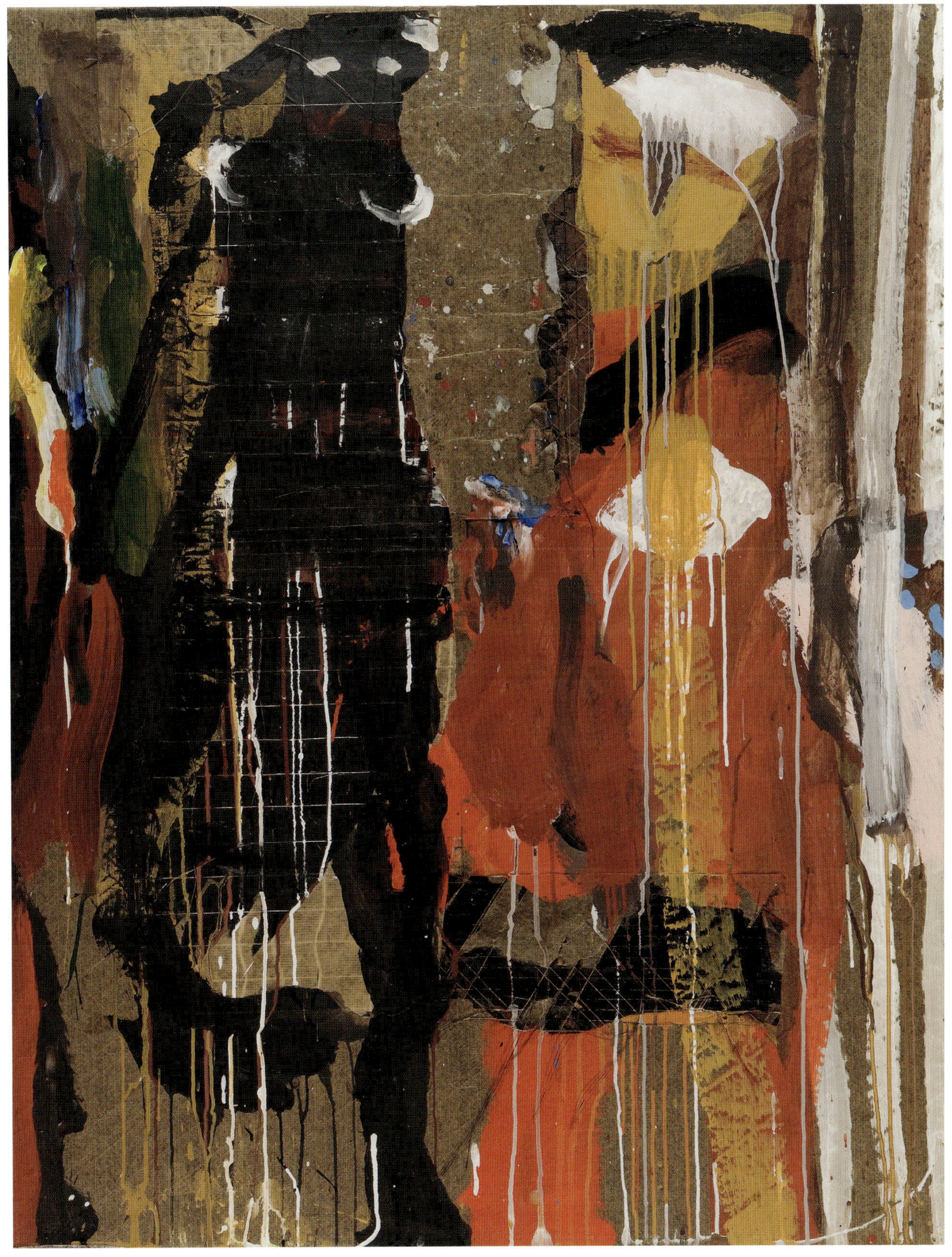

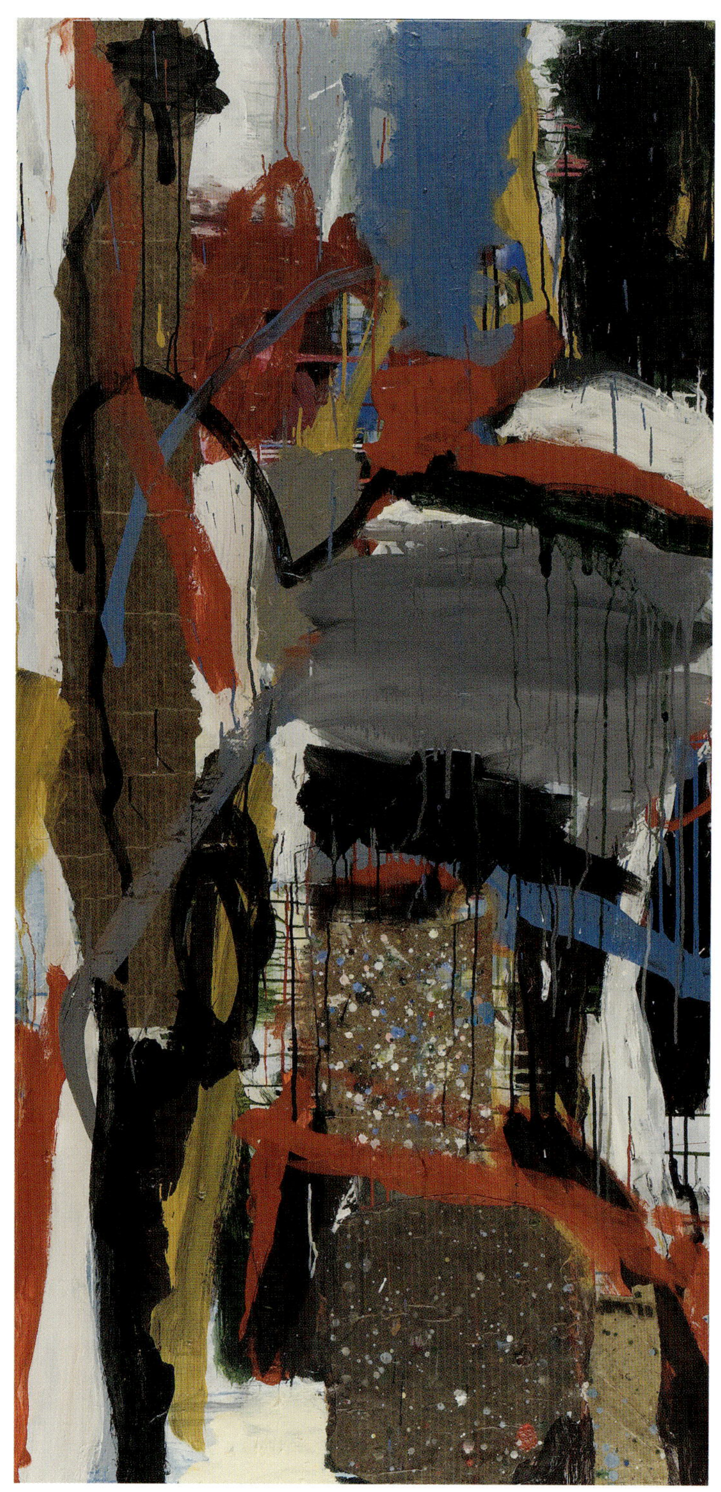

 Centauri 2012, acrylic and collage on linen, 120 x 92 cm. Courtesy Ann Thomson and Olsen Irwin Gallery, Sydney

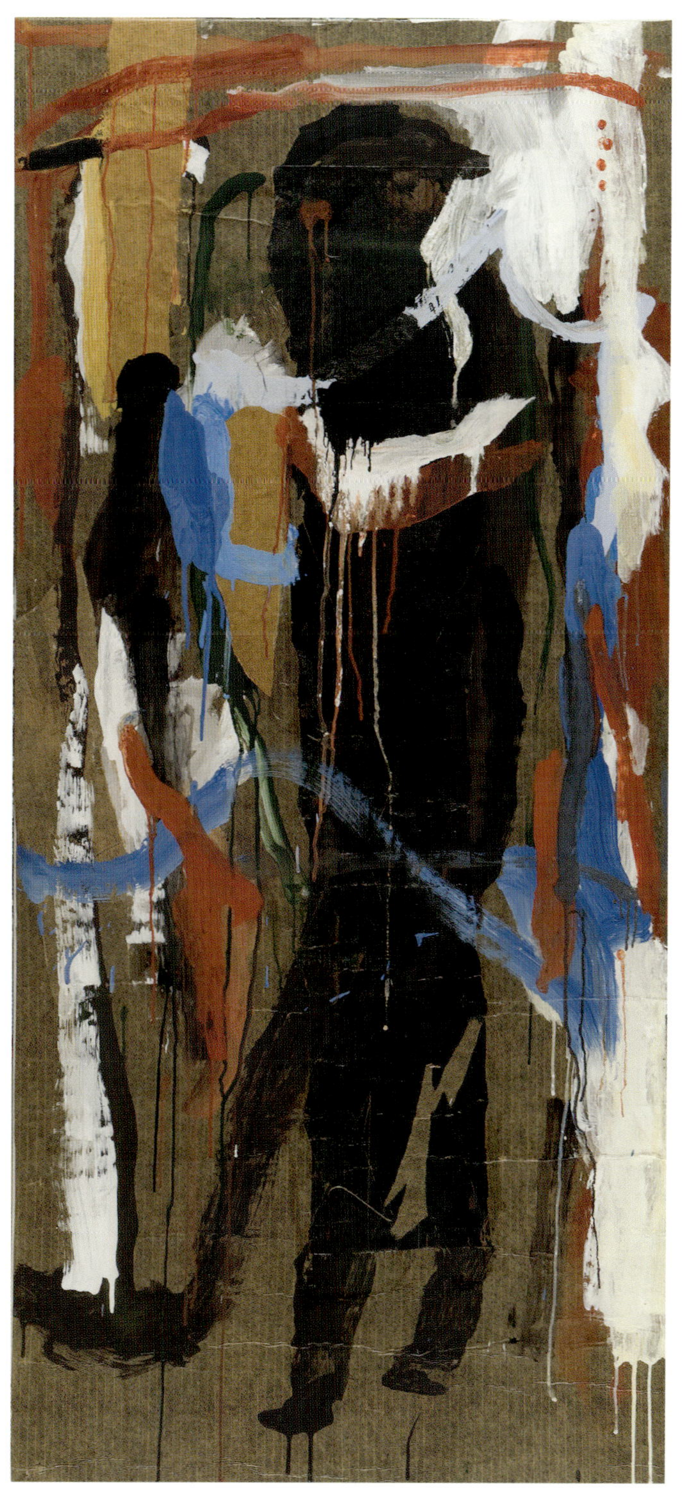

Magog 2011, acrylic and collage on linen, 180 x 81 cm. Courtesy Ann Thomson and Olsen Irwin Gallery, Sydney

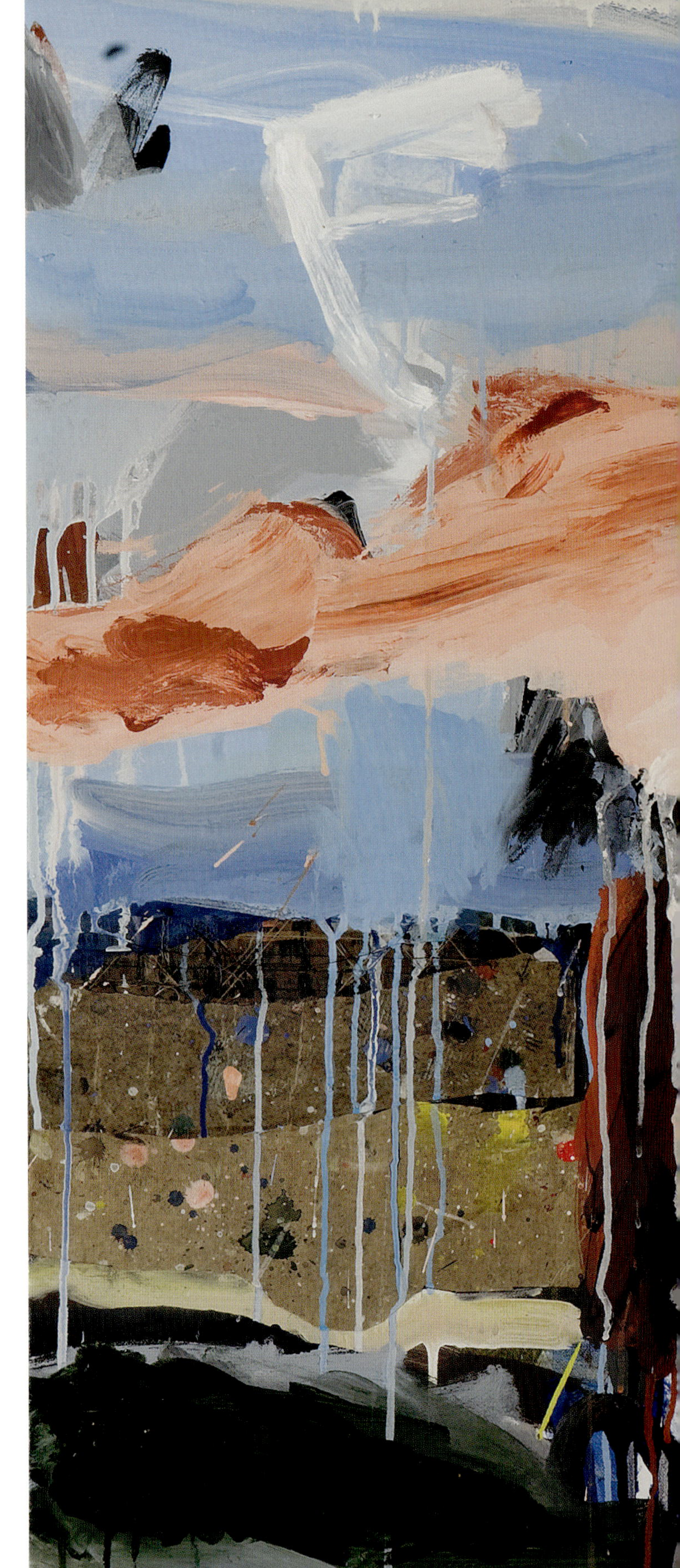

Utopia 2011, acrylic and collage on linen, 91cm x 122 cm
overleaf: *Water poised above water* 2014, acrylic on linen, 104 x 202 cm
both courtesy Ann Thomson and Olsen Irwin Gallery, Sydney

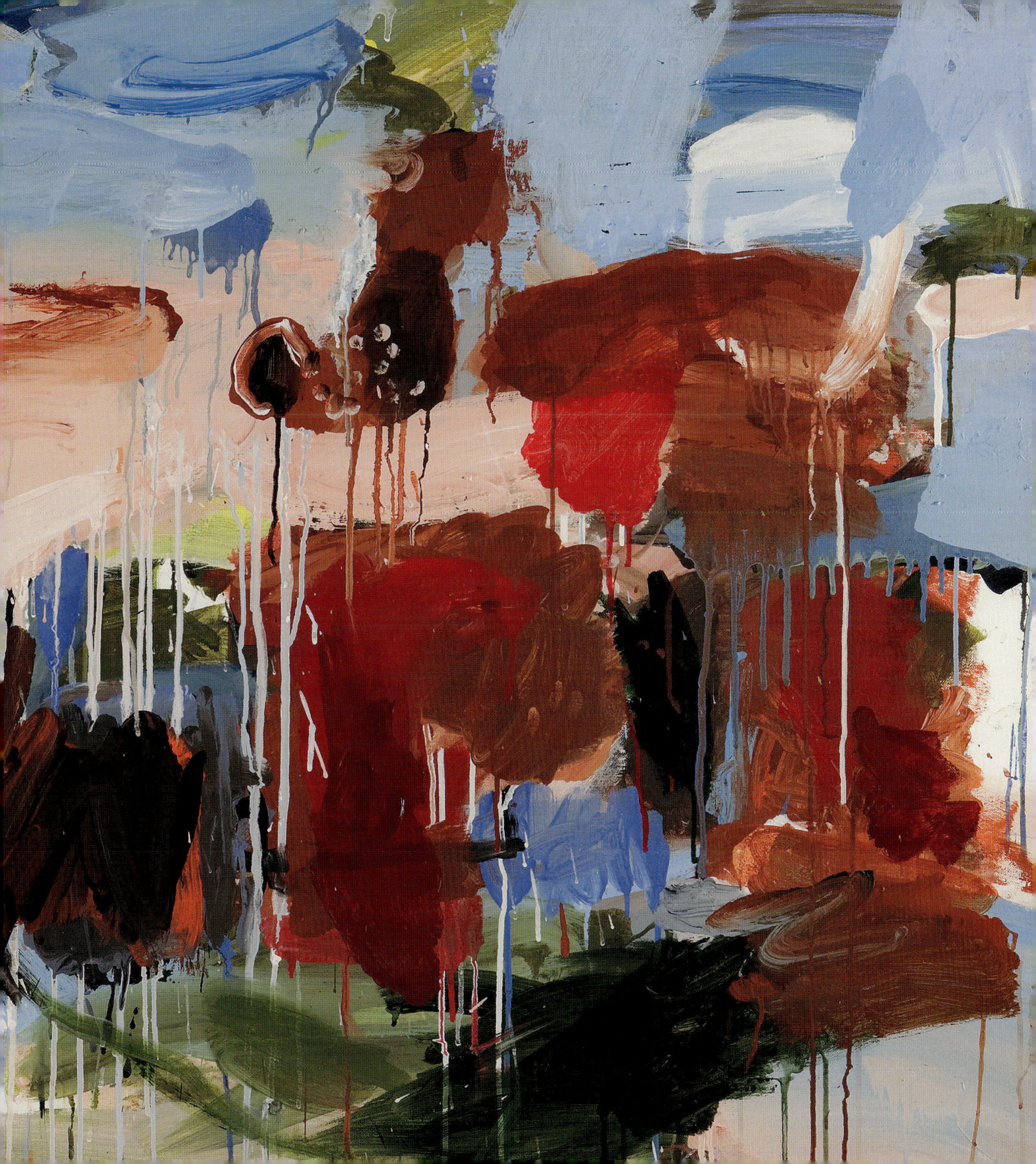

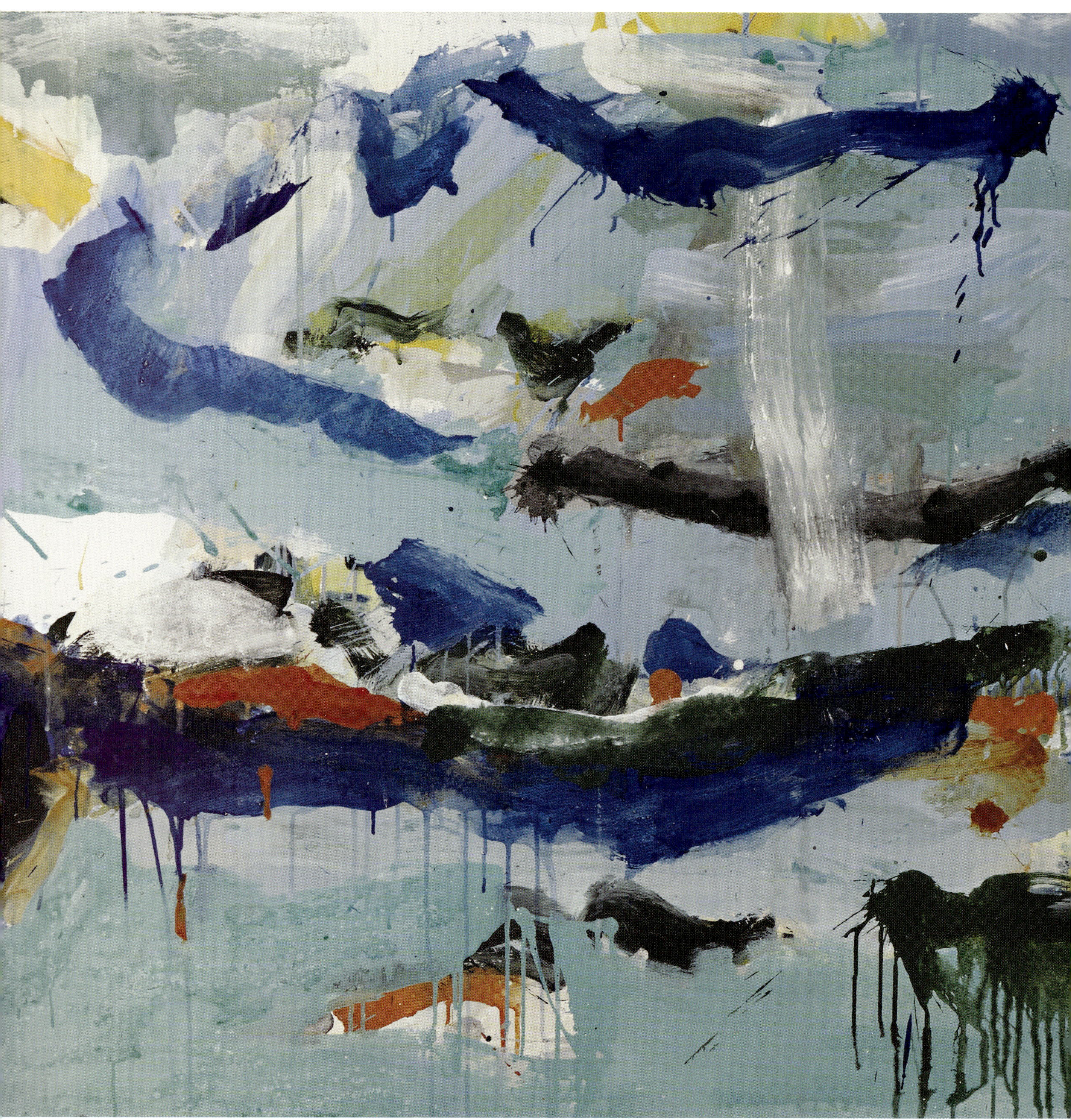

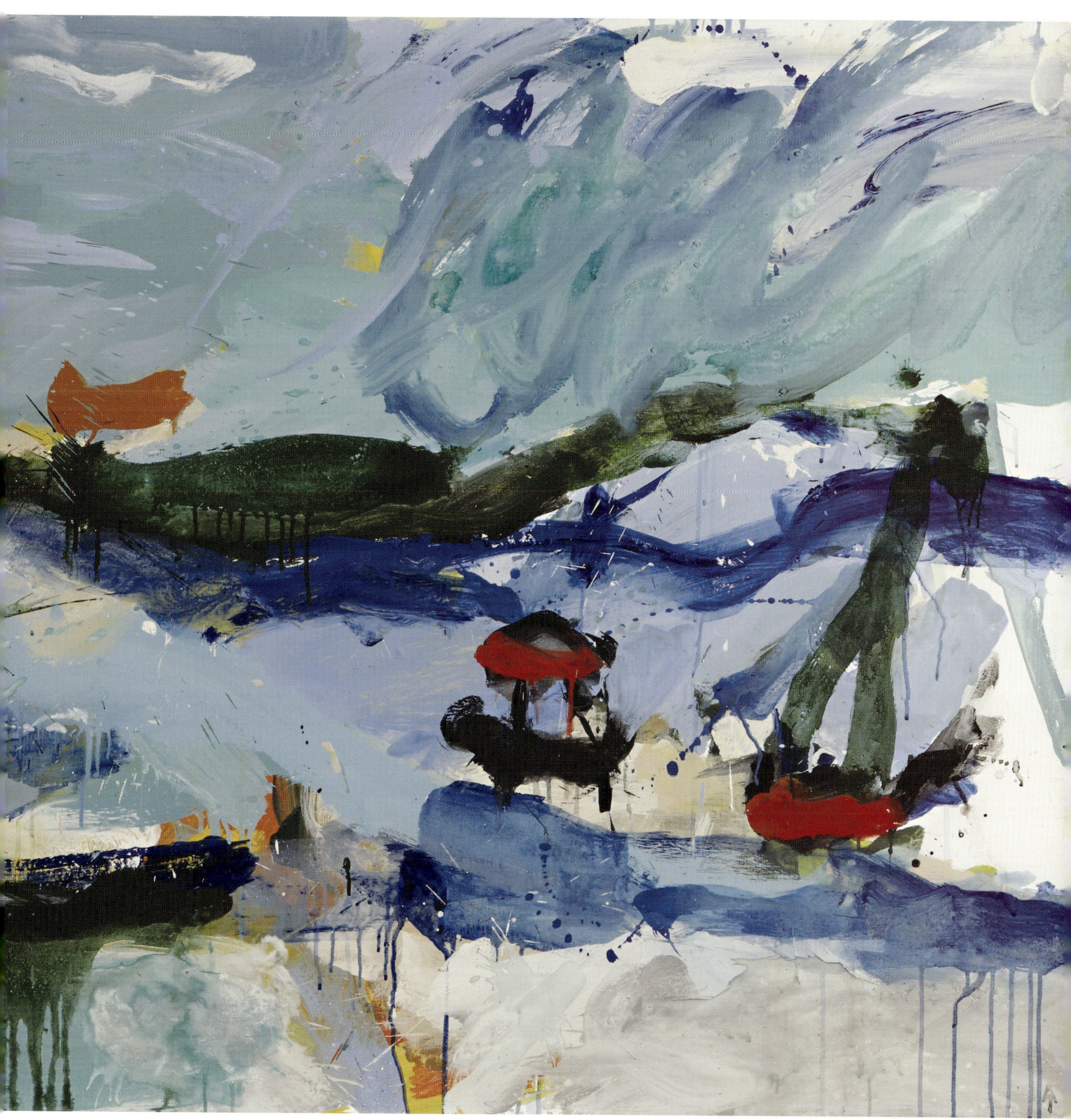

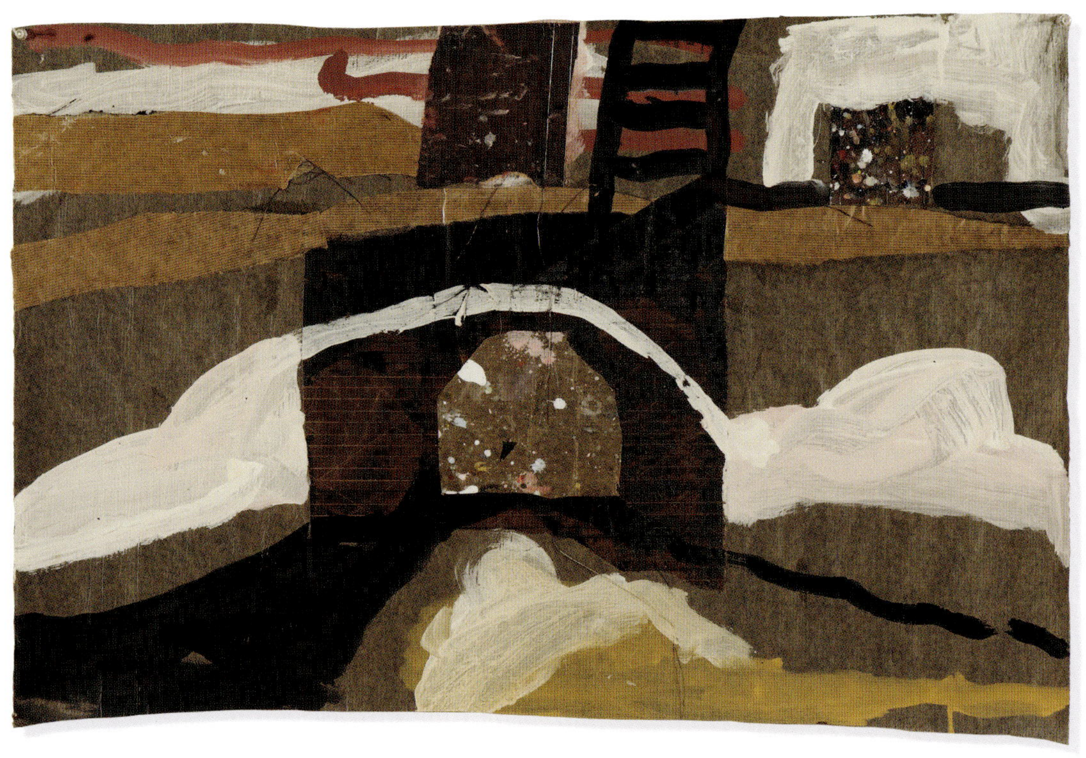

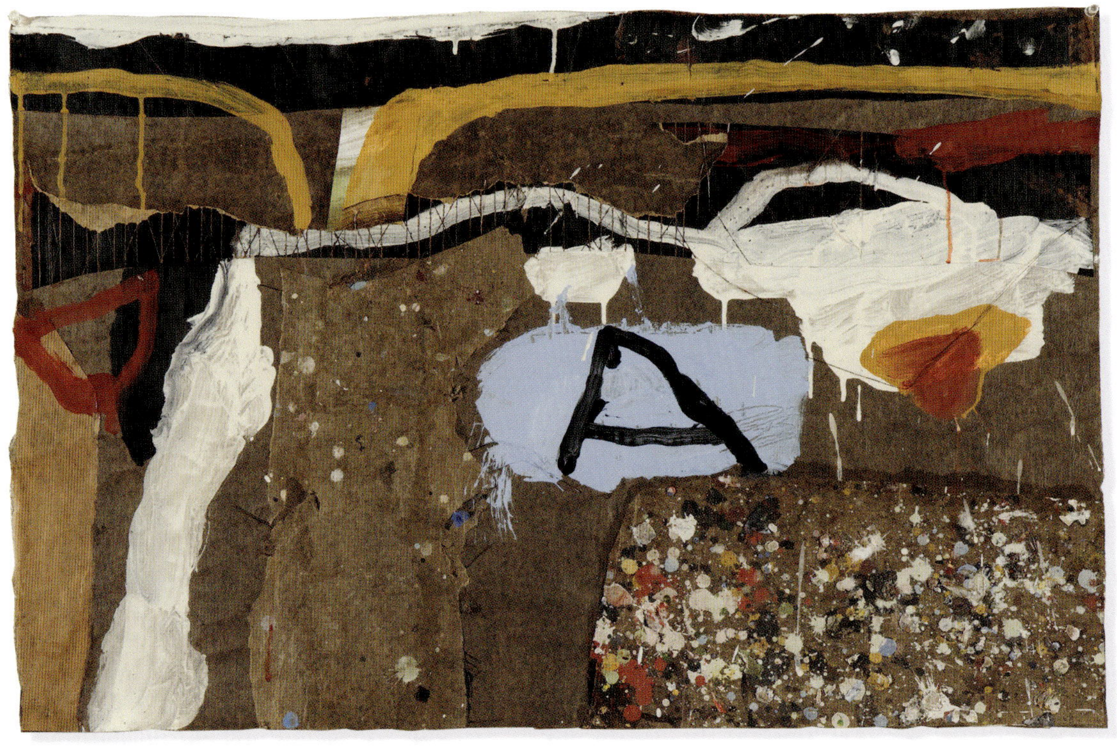

Half the night I & III 2011, acrylic on tarred paper, 58 x 88 cm. Private collection, Sydney

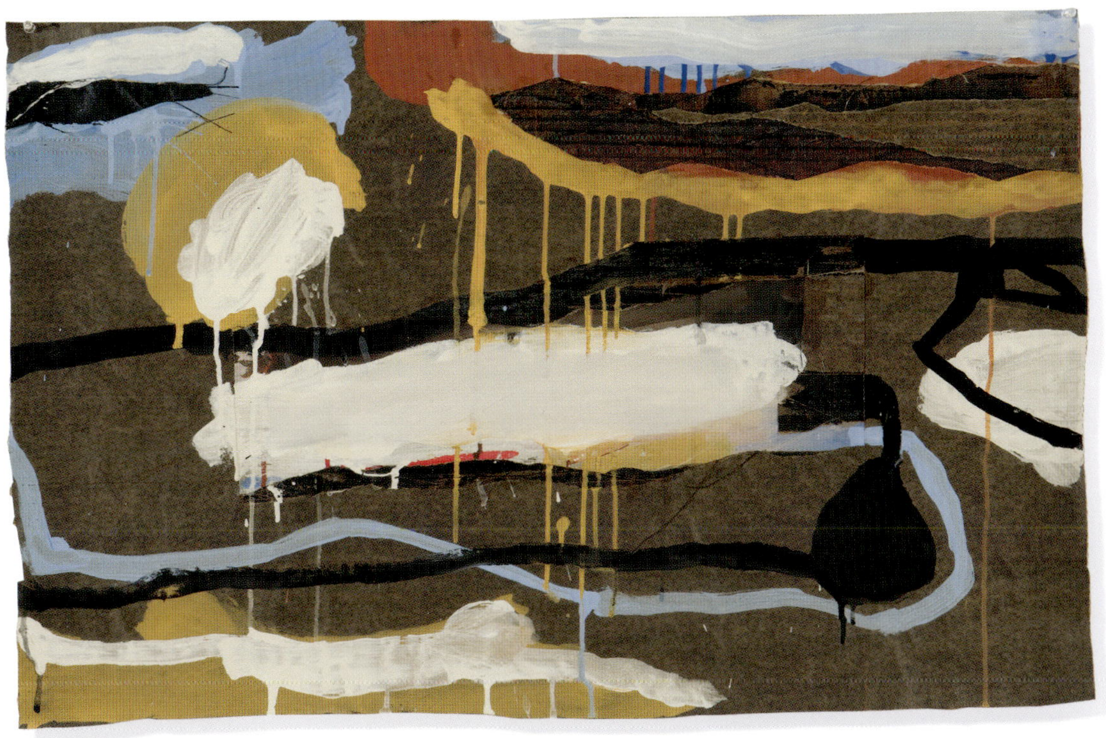

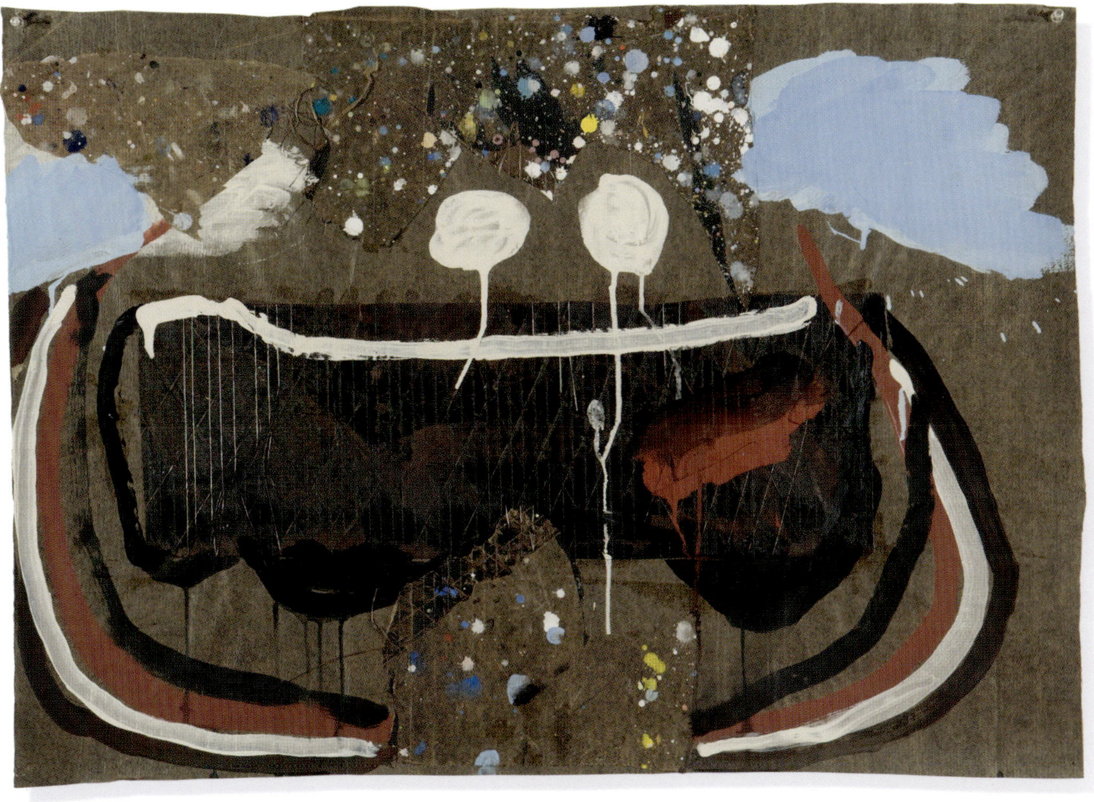

Half the night II & IV 2011, acrylic on tarred paper, 58 x 88 cm. Private collection, Sydney

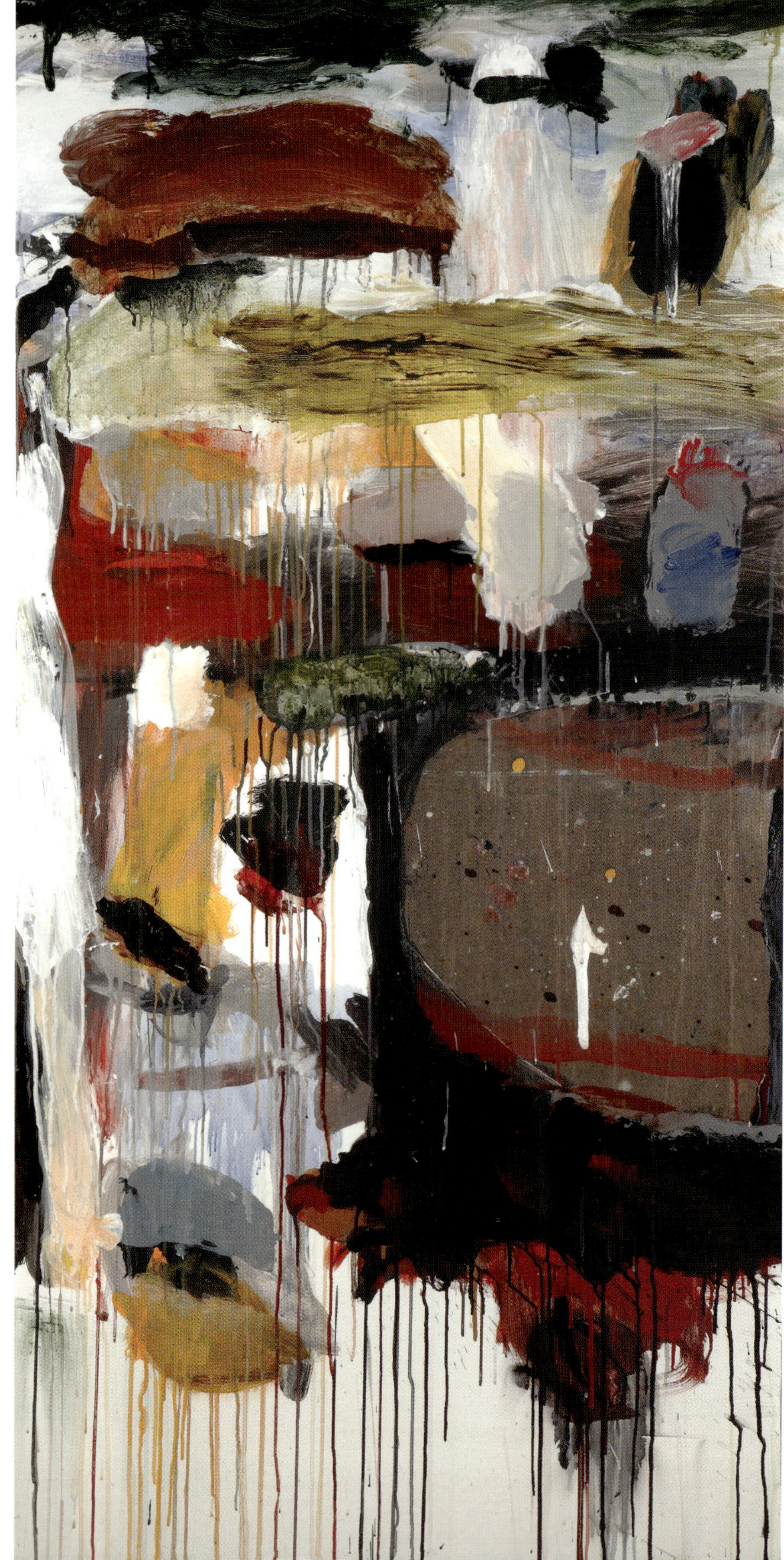

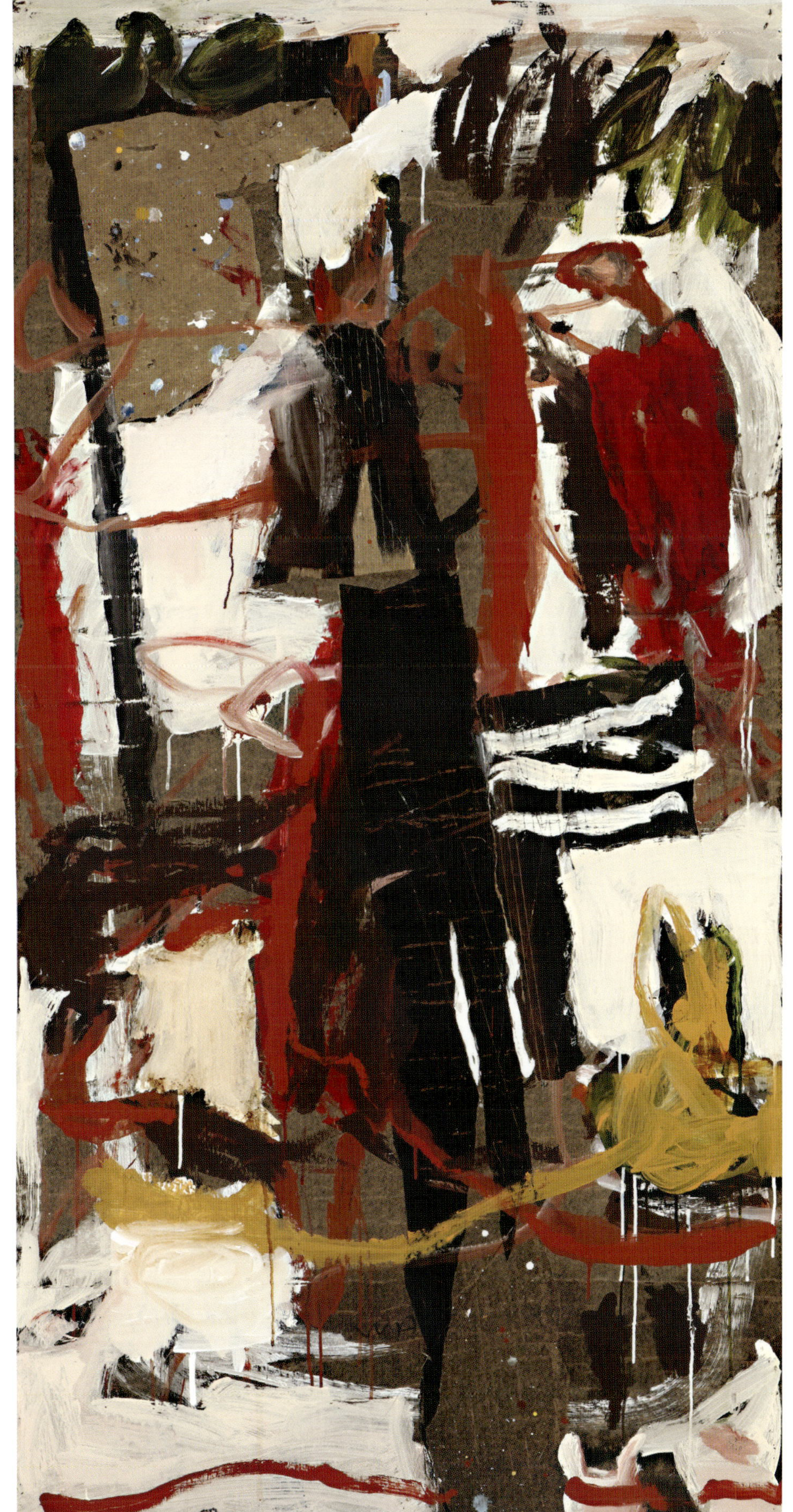

biographical note

Ann Thomson was born in Brisbane in 1933. After studying with Jon Molvig in the mid-1950s, she left Brisbane for Sydney to study at the National Art School in 1962. With the exception of a three year period spent in Brisbane (1974-1977), when she completed a 9-metre long mural commissioned for the University of Queensland's Malley Refectory, she has continued to live and work in Sydney. Since 1975 she has had periodic opportunities to work in Europe, especially in France.

Thomson's exhibiting career began in the mid-1960s when she held her first solo exhibition at Watters Gallery in Sydney. Since then her work has continued to be exhibited widely in Australia (Gallery A, Sydney; Christine Abrahams Gallery, Melbourne; Coventry Gallery, Sydney; Michael Milburn Gallery, Brisbane; Australian Galleries, Sydney; Charles Nodrum Gallery, Melbourne; Olsen Irwin, Sydney; Bruce Heiser Gallery, Brisbane) and abroad (Walter Bischoff Galerie, Berlin and Arts d'Australie Stéphane Jacob, Paris.)

Thomson's work has been curated in institutional exhibitions including *Landscape and Image, Contemporary Australian Art* in Indonesia (1978); Musee de l'Art Walloon, Liege, Belgium (1984); *Contemporary Australian Art*, The Warwick Arts Trust, London & Galleria Lillo, Venice (1985); *Surface for Reflexion*, AGNSW (1987); *Interpretations*, Goulburn Regional Gallery, NSW (1992); Lui Hat-su National Art Museum, Shanghai (1998); *Icarus*, Goulburn Regional Gallery, NSW (1999.)

In 1977 Thomson's work was the subject of a major exhibition at the Institute of Modern Art, Brisbane and in 1980 a survey exhibition of her work was curated by Monash University, Melbourne. *Australia Felix*, a major sculptural work, was commissioned and exhibited as the centrepiece of the Australian pavilion at the 1992 World Expo in Seville, Spain. This large-scale work was conceived to take advantage of the site's soaring eleven-metre ceiling. A year later, in 1993, *Australia Felix* was exhibited at the Art Gallery of New South Wales and the Australian National Maritime Museum, Sydney.

Ann Thomson won the Canberra Times National Arts Award in 1981. In 1984, her painting obtained the University of New South Wales Purchase Prize. In 1998 she was the recipient of the Wynne Prize, AGNSW. In 2002 she won the Geelong Contemporary Art Prize, and three years later in 2005 was awarded the Kedumba Drawing Award, NSW.

Her work is represented in major collections including the Thyssen-Bornemisza Collection, Madrid, Spain; Villa Haiss, Zell, Germany; National Gallery of Australia; Queensland Art Gallery; University Art Museum, University of Queensland; QUT Art Museum; Art Gallery of New South Wales; Parliament House Collection, Canberra; Griffith University Art Collection; Newcastle Region Art Gallery; and the Perc Tucker Regional Gallery, Townsville.

p 42 *Rough with age* 2010, acrylic and collage on linen, 166 x 82 cm. Courtesy Ann Thomson and Olsen Irwin Gallery, Sydney
p 43 *Tritone* 2012, acrylic on linen, 184 x 91 cm. Courtesy Ann Thomson and Olsen Irwin Gallery, Sydney
opposite: *Maja* 2014, acrylic and collage on linen, 153 x 122 cm. Courtesy Ann Thomson and Olsen Irwin Gallery, Sydney

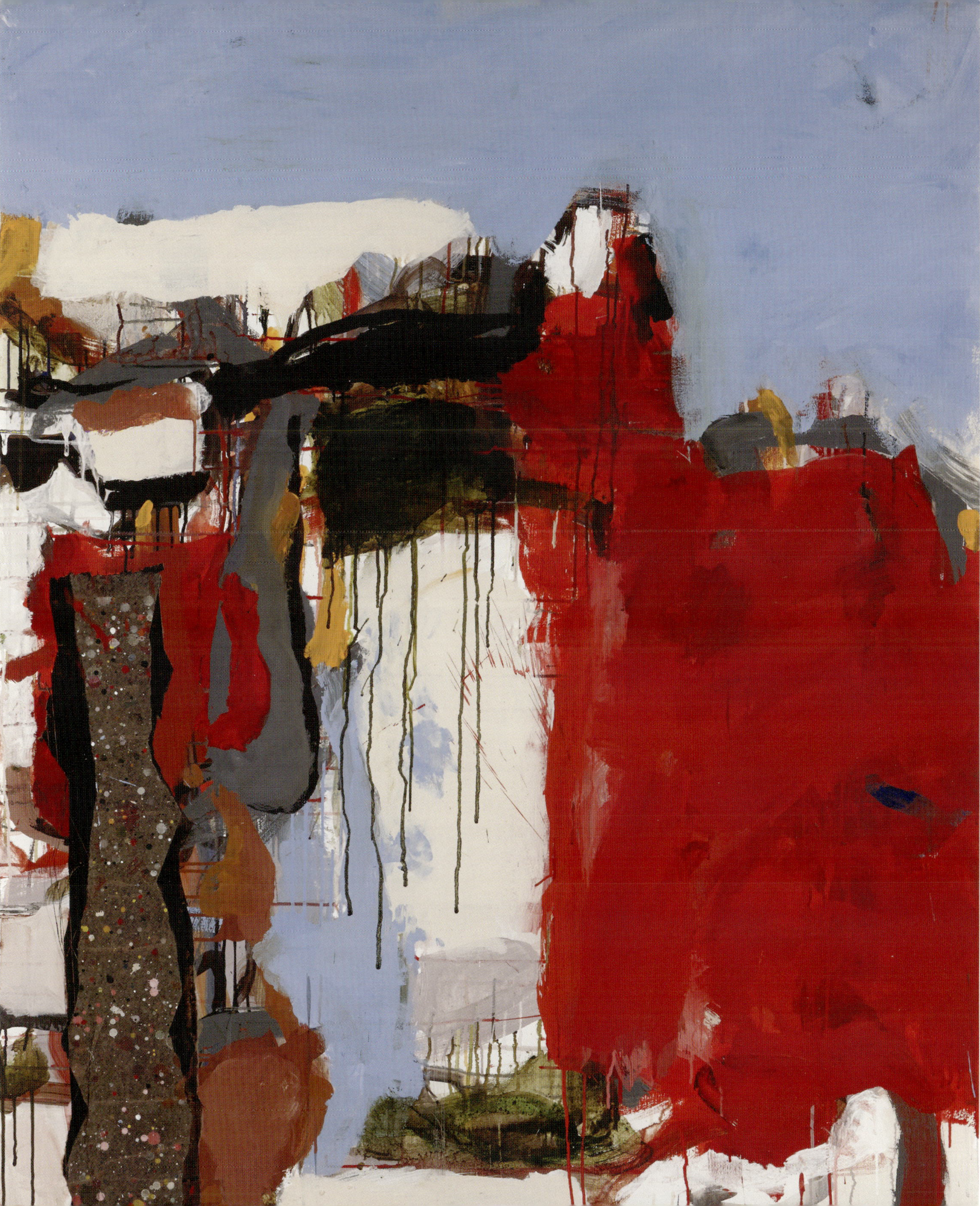

acknowledgements

The Drill Hall Gallery would like to thank Ann Thomson for her calm and constructive involvement in all stages of the preparation of this exhibition, and her generosity in making such a windfall of her recent works available. Our thanks also to the directors of the Olsen Irwin Gallery, Tim Olsen and Rex Irwin, for works they have lent from their gallery stock, and to their helpful staff: Anna Novochenok, Katrina Arendt and Brett Stone. There are several private lenders who prefer to remain anonymous — our thanks to them. David Malouf kindly consented to open the exhibtion. All scholarship pertaining to Ann Thomson is indebted to Anna Johnson's monograph *Ann Thomson* 2012, Tim Olsen Editions. Photography has been provided by Jenni Carter; Graham Maslen at Spitting Image supplied scans. Judith White and Michelle Monroe at the Art Gallery of New South Wales helped with the promotion of the exhibition in Sydney. Jeanette Brand designed the catalogue, invitations and banners. Tony Oates, David Boon, interns, volunteers and our installation crew have all contributed to the success of this exhibition.

Quotations from Jean Bazaine are taken from his book, *Le temps de la peinture*, Flammarion, 2002. The quotation from Valérie Zuchuat comes from her article "Jean Bazaine: le regard d'un peintre sur la peinture," in *Equinoxes,* issue 3, spring 2004 (http://www.brown.edu/Research/Equinoxes/journal/issue3/eqx3_zuchuat.html).

FREEHAND - RECENT WORKS BY ANN THOMSON
20 February - 5 April 2015

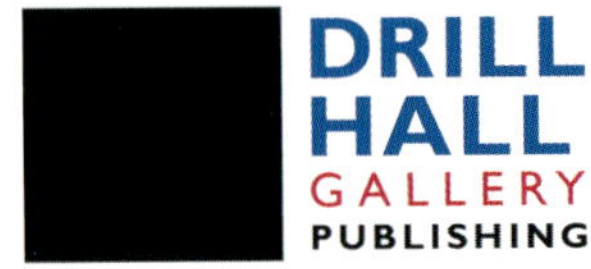

ISBN: 978-0-9942584-0-3
Texts: Terence Maloon
Catalogue design: Jeanette Brand
Printer: Union Offset
Photography: Jenni Carter

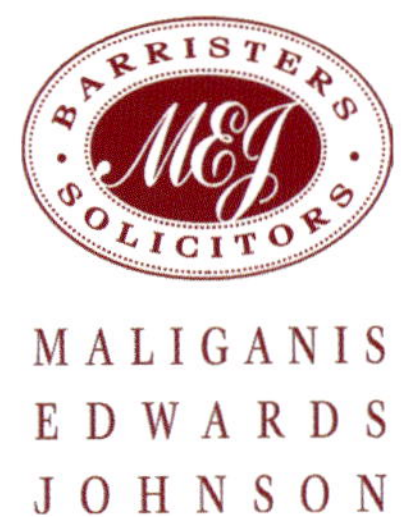

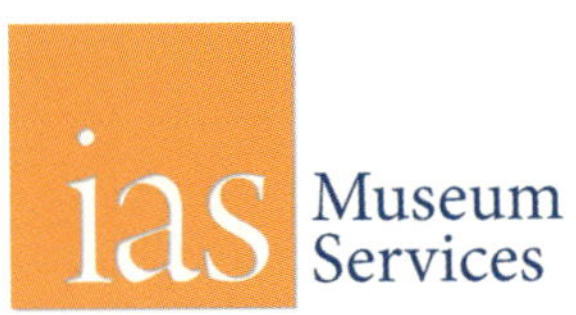

Director: Terence Maloon
Curator, Exhibitions: Tony Oates
Curator, Collection: David Boon
Manager, Outreach: Jeanette Brand
+ 61 2 6125 5832 dhg@anu.edu.au dhg.anu.edu.au

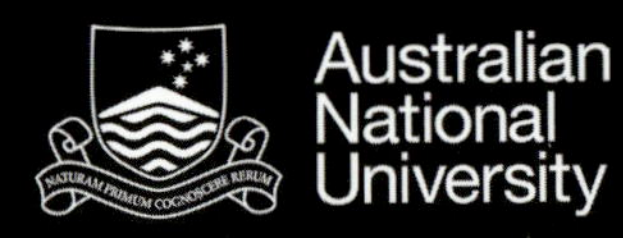